D1544935

MICROCOMPUTERS AND
THE SOCIAL STUDIES

GARLAND REFERENCE LIBRARY
OF SOCIAL SCIENCE
(VOL. 341)

MICROCOMPUTERS AND THE SOCIAL STUDIES
A Resource Guide for the
Middle and Secondary Grades

Joseph A. Braun, Jr.

GARLAND PUBLISHING, INC. • NEW YORK & LONDON
1986

Library of Congress Cataloging-in-Publication Data

Braun, Joseph A., 1947-
Microcomputers and the social studies.

(Garland reference library of social science ; v. 341)
Includes index.
1. Social sciences—Study and teaching—Data
processing. 2. Social sciences—Study and teaching—
Data processing—Bibliography. 3. Microcomputers.
I. Title. II. Series.
H62.B654   1986   300′.28′5416   86–25617
ISBN 0–8240–8579–5 (alk. paper)

Printed on acid-free, 250-year-life paper
Manufactured in the United States of America

To my daughter, Sage Elizabeth

As you grow, and, I hope, learn to appreciate the positive potential technology holds for humanity, keep in mind the words of the brave social studies teacher, Christa McAuliffe, whose life and tragic death touched the consciousness of the nation as this book was being written. As Christa often told her social studies students, never be afraid to "reach for the stars."

CONTENTS

PREFACE

When I informed a colleague that I was about to
undertake writing a reference guide on
microcomputers for social studies teachers he wrly
noted, "Given the current state of software
available, it will probably be a rather thin book."
This comment was made about a year and a half
before I submitted the manuscript to my editor. I
think my friend has been pleasantly surprised to
see all the developments in social studies
instruction as a result of the rapid increase in
software and applications of microcomputers. Thus,
my book is a bit thicker than my colleague
originally envisioned. I am sure that he would
agree with me that if the same rate of development
continues, a book written ten years from now on
social studies and microcomputers would have to be
bound in more than one volume.
      Since this book is intended to be a resource,
the reader may delve in almost anywhere. The book
has a variety of information that should be of
value to social studies instructors in several
ways. For those who have a minimal knowledge about
computers, there is some basic computer literacy
information. It can help social studies teachers
develop a better understanding of the history of
computers and how they are affecting education. It
can guide a teacher in making an informed choice
about what software to purchase. It can help the
teacher use widely recognized social education
strategies in conjunction with the computer.
Finally, teachers can glean ideas for dealing with
current curriculum issues such as how are computers
affecting our society now and in the future.
      Since most social studies teachers have an
inherent love of history as a discipline this
seemed like a logical starting point in a reference
guide. Chapter 1 traces humanity's interest in

computing and chronicles the efforts of early
pioneers who created devices to assist efforts at
performing calculations mechanically. Chapter 2
continues the narrative historical account and
begins with the phenomenal rate of development, and
miniaturization, of the computer and its various
parts which has occurred in the past 25 years. The
second part of this chapter is a primer on the
computer, its components, and how they function as
a system. The discussion here is limited to school
uses; such recent developments as laser printers,
which are currently well beyond the budget of most
school districts, are not included. Descriptions of
the various types of courseware and strategies for
their evaluation are identified in Chapter 3. Also
described are instruments that have been developed
by professional organizations including the
National Council for the Social Studies.

      For those who are more interested in
information on specific programs, Chapter 4 is an
annotated bibliography of social studies
courseware. The heart of this book lies in the
final three chapters. They contain some of the most
current information available at the time of this
printing. Chapter 5 begins with a brief distinction
made between computer assisted instruction and
computer managed instruction. The author recognizes
that some authorities in the field have devised
other criteria for classifying different types of
software. Thus, I tried to develop as comprehensive
a model for classifying software as I could, based
on the literature. Databases are covered in the
next section. Chapter 6 is an annotated
bibliography of software for computer managed
instruction. This includes teacher utility programs
as well as databases that are appropriate for
social studies instruction. The final chapter
considers social education issues as they relate to
the microcomputer. The three themes addressed are
artificial intelligence and its relationship to
human consciousness, values education, and
computers and lifestyles of the future.

      The afterword describes the efforts of Jack
Taub, the creator of the THE SOURCE, a leading
information utility, to develop an Education
Utility. When it becomes operational, this
development in educational computing could
revolutionize social studies instruction as well as

that in other subject areas. Its impact on
education and learning could be a breakthrough of
the same magnitude as Johan Gutenberg's invention
of movable type.

There are many people who contributed in a
variety of ways to my efforts in completing this
book and I would like to acknowledge their
contributions. Barry VanDemeen, educational
director of the Chicago Museum of Science and
Industry, helped me acquire many of the
photographs. Jean Johnson, the extension reference
librarian at the University of Wyoming, helped me
trace down innumerable references. Several software
authors and publishers were gracious in providing
me with examples of their products and I have
acknowledged them in appropriate sections in the
text, but I would particularly like to thank David
Dockterman of Tom Snyder Productions, Walter Koetke
of Scholastic, Inc., and Dr. Tom Switzer of the
University of Michigan, who helped me obtain
prototypes of their software and documentation
while they were still under development. Sally
Cornish of the World Future Society and Charles
Rivera, editor of Social Education, were kind
enough to give me permission to reproduce documents
from their journals. Several people consented to
read and critique sections of the manuscript and I
would like to thank Dr. Dorothy Seaberg, Dr. Robert
Morissette, Terry Bottorff, and Malcolm Cook for
taking time out of their busy schedules to offer me
their suggestions. Dennis Gooler, former Dean of
the College of Education at Northern Illinois
University, my alma mater, graciously provided me
with the information reported in the Afterword. The
Computer Company of Cheyenne Wyoming was most
helpful in obtaining necessary equipment and
supplies used in the production of this book. Renee
Reese, my secretary, was of great assistance in the
preparation of the final manuscript. My editor,
Marie Ellen Larcada, deserves a special note of
thanks for answering my countless questions and
providing me with the support, encouragement, and
emendations necessary to see this project come to
fruition. Thanks also to Marie Ellen for all the
tips and encouragement she gave me in the first
years of being a parent. Finally, I would like to
thank my wife, Anne Gosch, because she has
contributed in so many ways. Not only did she

contribute her talents by creating graphics, she also tirelessly reviewed each chapter as it was prepared. Most importantly, Anne provided the love and affection that sustained me at those times when I needed them most.

Microcomputers and the Social Studies

CHAPTER 1

FROM BEADS TO BITS

If the musings of science fiction writers were possible and people could travel through time, imagine the reaction of an Assyrian merchant who is transported from his dusty, primitive marketplace to our twentieth-century version, the up-to-date supermarket. Much of what he would see would be astounding, and at least one activity would be completely baffling, computing the cost of a purchase. As he stood in line he would observe the salesclerk take each item and pass it over a light sensitive device that automatically notes the cost. The price is tallied by machine and a voice synthesizer reports the amount to the clerk and shopper. All of this is possible because of a product of modern living, the electronic computer. Things were certainly different back in his day and age!

For a great deal of human history transactions that took place in marketplaces did not use currency as a medium of exchange. More often than not bartering and an exchange of goods was the process for conducting business. Thus, a chicken might be traded for a pile of vegetables or piece of fabric. Our Assyrian visitor did not need a written system for performing mathematical operations to arrive at a total sale or keep track of inventory. In fact, a written method for performing mathematics did not appear for almost a millennium after the decline of Assyrian civilization. In ancient times an individual who needed to perform calculations used a rudimentary, nonelectrical form of a computer, the abacus.

This chapter provides historical background about the computer. The first attempts at constructing computing devices and the advancement of mathematics as a science are concurrent stories. The dreams, schemes, and lives of those individuals who played a significant role in the development of

computing devices will be recounted. By examining
the lives of those who played a role in developing
computers, the social studies teacher can help
students view computers from a historical
perspective. Such a perspective enables the youth
of today to appreciate the fact that computers,
although not powered by electricity, have been part
of human civilization much longer than most would
guess.

ANTIQUITY'S COMPUTER

While many assume it was of Chinese origin,
the fact is no one knows exactly where the abacus,
or counting board, originated. The etymology of the
word can be traced to the Phoencian "abak," which
means board or tablet. Some speculate that the word
may have descended from the ancient Hebrew, "ibeq,"
which means "to wipe the dust." In its earliest
form, this is an apt description of how numbers
were counted. Shallow grooves or lines in the
ground were traced and pebbles, stones, or bits of
bone were used as counters. Obviously, there are no
surviving examples of these earliest computing
devices. Anthropologists have, however, unearthed
small round stones used as counters from the ruins
of ancient Babylonia.
It is simple to see the evolution of counters
to the actual abacus. The small stones or bits of
bone were strung on wires, or coarse hair, and
contained within a frame in an ordered pattern.
Herodotus describes pebble abacuses in the fifth
century B.C. and explains how the interest on a
loan of 766 talents, 1,095 drachmas, and 5 obols
over a period of 1,464 days, at the rate of one
drachma a day for 5 talents was calculated.
The Greeks, Babylonians, and other
civilizations of antiquity had written numbering
systems although they were not designed for
reckoning. In general, the systems were complex and
awkward to write. They lacked the concept of zero
and fixed numerical places for tens, hundreds,
thousands, etc. These written numerical systems
were not intended for computation, but rather for
reporting the results of calculations arrived at
through manipulating an abacus. Try calculating the
product of the Roman numbers MDCCLVI by LIX. This
difficult problem is rendered quite simple with the

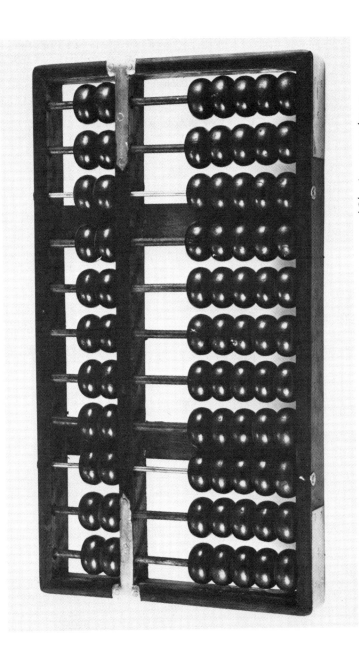

An abacus—the oldest of computing devices. (Photo courtesy of IBM Archives)

aid of an abacus.

With an abacus a prerequisite knowledge of a
numerical system is not necessary. For centuries
most everyday arithmetic problems were solved by
uneducated traders and merchants with this
primitive computer. Thus, the abacus was an
indispensable and commonplace tool in most Western,
as well as Eastern, cultures.

On a Roman abacus, each wire holds ten or more
"calculi" representing units, tens, hundreds, and
so forth. When the number of "calculi" on one wire
exceeds ten, one is carried over to the next wire
to the left. The ancient Chinese used bamboo rods
in place of beads or pebbles. They added a crossbar
separating two zones on the frame - one called
"heaven" and the other called "earth." The heaven
zone contained two beads each of which was worth
five. The earth beads stand for one. At the outset
the operator places the beads towards the outside
portion of the frame. The beads are moved towards
the crossbeam to represent numbers and perform
calculations.

The abacus, then, took several forms depending
on the numbering system of the culture. The use of
an abacus as a computing device would be prevalent
today if it were not for a remarkable discovery of
the Hindus, the zero, which would eventually
revolutionize mathematics.

THE REVOLUTIONARY IMPACT OF ZERO AND OTHER
ADVANCES IN MATHEMATICS

The exact date of the Hindu invention of zero
is not recorded, but the first unquestioned use of
it is 876 A.D. It was through the Arabs, who had
considerable commercial dealings with India, that
the use of a decimal system which included zero
spread to Western Europe. The Hindu-Arabic system
of numeration flowed with the tide of the Moorish
invasions. Its spread can be traced through Africa,
Spain, and Italy.

While its simplicity is obvious in comparison
to the Roman, the widespread use of the
Hindu-Arabic system of notation moved at an
incredibly slow pace. Surprisingly, the transition
from Roman to Hindu-Arabic numerals did not occur
until somewhere between the thirteenth and
seventeenth centuries in most regions of Germany,

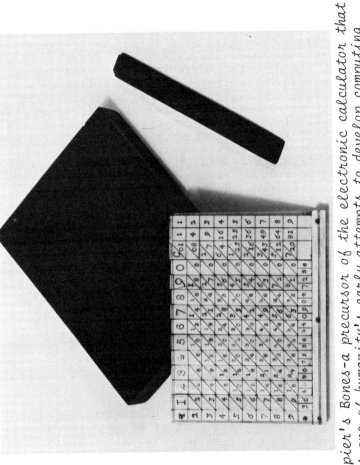

Napier's Bones—a precursor of the electronic calculator that was one of humanity's early attempts to develop computing devices. (Photo courtesy IBM Archives)

France, and England. In fact, in 1299 the merchants of Florence were forbidden by law to use the new symbols in reckoning their accounts. As with many advances in civilization, such as indoor plumbing or mechanical clocks in the home, the use of the Hindu-Arabic system followed social class lines. It was first acquired by the nobility and then eventually trickled down to lower social classes. Thus, despite the ease with which pen or mental arithmetic could be computed by the Hindu-Arabic system, the counting board and Roman numeration remained popular with the masses. As late as 1636 the mayor's audits for the city of Bristol were reported using Roman numerals. This resistance and slow pace of change seem remarkable when compared with the rapid spread of microcomputers during the closing decades of this century.

In 1614 a milestone in the advancement of mathematics, which would eventually have a good deal of influence on the development of computers, was put forth by a Scottish baron. John Napier worked out a system based on the geometric progression of powers relative to the number 1, which he called logarithms, or more simply logs.

Toward the end of his life, Napier created a hands-on approach to multiplication tables with a set of four-sided, numbered rods. Napier's Rods, or bones as they are sometimes referred to, were essentially a multiplication table cut up into movable columns. Though not particularly efficient, Napier's Rods proved immensely popular and were widely used throughout Europe. Even the lower end of the multiplication tables taxed the ability of well-educated people at this time since arithmetic was not typically included in the curriculum of most schools.

Napier's initial work with logarithms was continued by an Oxford scholar of geometry, Henry Briggs. Having begun three years after Napier's work was published, by the end of his life Briggs had calculated logarithmic tables of numbers up to 100,000. The idea of using logarithms was accepted immediately, and soon resulted in another manipulative device, the slide rule, which remained popular with scientists and mathematicians for centuries. An English clergyman, William Oughtred is credited with the invention of this clever device in 1621. It is interesting to note that with

the creation of the microprocessing chip and the
development of the hand-held calculator, the slide
rule is rapidly becoming an antique.

We can readily see the impact that these
computing devices had on western civilization. In
the middle of the fifteenth century Prince Henry
the Navigator established a fortress, which served
as a navigational research institute, atop the
cliffs of Sargres on the coast of Portugal. It was
here that the latest navigational devices such as
the quadrant and the cross-staff were developed.
These devices are computers of sorts since they
measure the relationship between quantities,
namely, the altitude of stars and the elevation of
the sun, which can then be correlated to yield the
distance a ship has traveled. These devices ushered
in the Age of Exploration and European recognition
of a western hemisphere.

Prior to the application of electricity to
digital computers, there were several other
noteworthy mechanical calculators that performed
mathematical operations and compiled quantities,
which influenced the development of the computer
that we know today.

THE ADVENT OF MECHANICAL CALCULATORS

For several centuries historians mistakenly
credited the invention of the first mechanical
calculator to the famous French philosopher and
mathematician, Blaise Pascal. While Pascal did make
an important contribution to the field, which we
will take up later, the work of a twentieth-century
German historian has correctly identified Wilhelm
Schickard as the first inventor of a mechanical
calculator in 1623, the year Pascal was born. How
could historians have overlooked Schickard's
contribution for so long ?

Wilhelm Schickard, as was typical of
intellectuals influenced by the Renaissance,
cultivated a wide variety of interests including
mathematics, optics, cartography, linguistics,
meteorology, and astronomy. After attending the
University of Tübingen he was awarded a
professorship there in Hebrew and Oriental
languages. It was during his tenure that he was
introduced to and became a close friend of
astronomer Johannes Kepler. It was this

relationship that gave Shickard his place in history.

A great personal and professional affinity developed between the two men, despite the fact that Kepler was twenty-four years Schickard's senior. Through conversations and correspondence Schickard and Kepler discussed the scientific and mathematical achievements of the day, such as logarithms and Napier's rods. Motivated in part by his ability to work with his hands, Schickard designed and built a computing device that he called the Calculating Clock sometime in 1623.

In a letter to Kepler, Schickard detailed the results of his efforts. He placed an order with a local craftsman to construct a Calculating Clock for his friend, Kepler. But before work could be completed Schickard's quarters caught fire destroying the half-completed machine. Before he could resume work on another, Schickard fell victim to the plague.

Five years before his development of the Calculating Clock, the Thirty Years War broke out and the campaigns of the emerging nation states were raging across continental Europe. With the armies came disease such as bubonic plague. Schickard and his entire family were among its victims. It is speculated that Schickard's possessions were either burned or looted, a common occurrence to the property of families afflicted with the plague. Thus, we have no actual trace of his invention.

It is only through his letters to Kepler that we have any record of Schickard's accomplishments. Curiously, scholars overlooked Schickard's description and drawings of the Calculating Clock among the voluminous body of correspondence that Kepler left. It wasn't until 1935 when one of Kepler's biographers, Franz Hammer, pieced together a description and drawing of the Calculating Clock that we knew of its existence. Finally, in 1960 through the drawing and letters that he wrote to Kepler, a workable reconstruction of Schickard's invention was completed. This incredible example of the fruits of historical research, the reconstruction of the Calculating Clock, is on display at the Deutsches Museum in Munich. Thus, it was over three hundred years later, after a reconstruction had been completed from one of

Schickard's letters, that he has assumed his
rightful place in the history of computers.

For centuries, then, Blaise Pascal had been
mistakenly credited with the invention of the first
mechanical calculator. The accomplishments of this
remarkable man, among which was the development of
a mechanical calculator, are worth noting. As a
child he proved several fundamental mathematical
theorems. He is credited with the explanation of a
basic principle of hydraulics, Pascal's law -
irrespective of the source of pressure on a
contained liquid, the effect of that pressure will
be transmitted with equal force in every direction.
He is also credited with the invention of the
hydraulic press and the syringe. Truly a genius, it
is indeed sad that he died at the early age of
thirty-nine of ulcers and stomach cancer, the
result of a tormented personal life. Remarkable as
his life was, if he had lived longer, his
accomplishments would have been astounding.

Several years before his death, Blaise Pascal
did mechanize a calculating device to aid his
father. When the Thirty Years War commenced, France
reneged on a substantial part of its national debt.
Facing bankruptcy, since he had invested heavily in
municipal bonds, the senior Pascal secured an
assignment as a tax commissioner in upper Normandy.
Disgusted with the laborious task of using the
abacus to count tax levies, Blaise set about to
design a digital computing machine. Through a
careful design of weighted rachets, gears, and
axles Pascal developed a six-digit adding machine,
the Pascaline. Unfortunately, because of the low
quality of metalwork at this time, the Pascaline
was prone to malfunction. Coupled with a high price
tag of a hundred pounds, which represented a year's
income to the middle class, the Pascaline never
caught on. The aristocracy, to whom Pascal thought
the machine would appeal as a novelty, had little
use for numeracy. To the aristocracy numeracy was
synonymous with bookkeeping, the work of servants.
Unlike Schickard's calculator, several Pascalines
found their way into museums and are preserved.

A final character to make a significant
contribution to the development of computers during
this time was Gottfried Wilhelm von Leibniz. Like
his contemporaries, Schickard and Pascal, Leibniz
was also a child prodigy who developed numerous

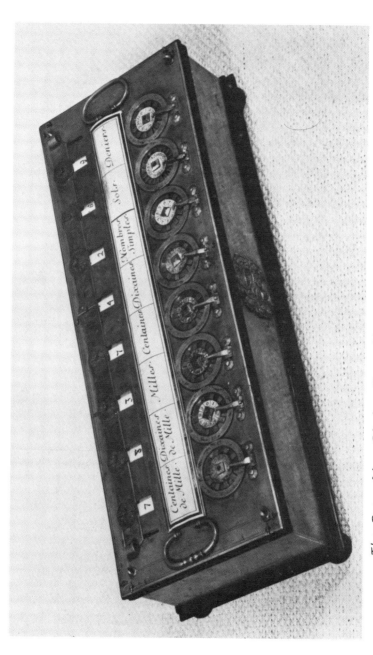

The Pascaline-Blaise Pascal's contribution to computing devices. (Photo courtesy of IBM Archives)

interests and talents. Leibniz left the world a
lofty legacy of achievement before succumbing to
chronic gout at the age of seventy.

Considered one of the most profound of
philosopher-scientists of modern times, Leibniz
created differential calculus. Because of intense
nationalistic pride, British mathematicians of the
time promulgated the notation of Newton rather than
Leibniz, a German. Leibniz induced Louis XIV to
construct a Suez canal. Leibniz championed the use
of the vernacular over Latin in the Berlin Academy
which he helped establish. For our purposes, the
most noteworthy of his creations was the Stepped
Reckoner.

The key to the Stepped Reckoner was a special
gear, called the Leibniz wheel, which acted as a
mechanical multiplier. Actually a metal cylinder
with nine horizontal rows of teeth, the Reckoner
consisted of eight Leibniz wheels connected by a
central shaft. A single turn of the shaft rotated
all eight cylinders, which displayed the answers.
Capable of processing fairly large numbers,
multiplicands of eleven or more digits, the
Reckoner wasn't fully automatic and required human
help to carry and borrow digits. Considered a more
sophisticated computer than the Calculating Clock
or the Pascaline, the machines were custom made and
rare until the beginning of the nineteenth century
when descendents of the Reckoner became popular
business calculators. It is interesting to note
that until the electronic calculator, most business
calculators operated on the principles and wheel
that Leibniz worked out.

All three of these pioneers in the development
of early computers made important conceptual
advances in applying technology to the process of
calculating. Interestingly, the lives of Schickard,
Pascal, and Leibniz contain noteworthy
similarities. First, a strong Renaissance influence
is evident in their wide range of interests and
abilities. And second, they all showed considerable
gifts and talents at early ages. We will see these
same patterns in the lives of other important
contributors to the development of computers.

Encouraging interest in many areas of learning
for all students and an awareness of the importance
of identifying those that are truly gifted and
talented should be concerns of social studies

Leibniz's Stepped Recknor was conceptually a remarkable device. (Photo courtesy of IBM Archives)

educators. Social studies and well-roundedness go
hand in hand. While every child has gifts and
talents, some have more than others. We should try
to identify those students in our classes who
possess unusual talent or interest in unique areas,
particularly with regard to social studies
applications and microcomputers. These students may
be the Schickards, Pascals, and Leibnizes of the
future.

The next important figure to play a role in
the history of computing was also gifted and
talented. The Renaissance ideal also deeply
influenced him. Unfortunately, he was also a tragic
and pathetic figure. His times are characterized as
the zenith of the industrial revolution. It was a
period of great inventiveness, social class
development, and accomplishment in the world of
arts and letters.

BRIDGES BETWEEN THE INDUSTRIAL REVOLUTION AND THE INFORMATION AGE

Charles Babbage was the son of a neurotic
father but apparently normal mother to whom he was
devoted. Babbage was born in Devonshire, England,
on December 26, 1791. As a youth he was quite frail
and extremely bright. A graduate of Trinity
College, Cambridge, Babbage dabbled in the occult.
More importantly, while still a university student,
Babbage attacked the Analytical Society, the most
distinguished association of British
mathematicians, regarding their adherence to Sir
Issac Newton's approach to calculus notation. His
attack took the form of a parody that he published
regarding the notation system of Newton. Babbage
believed Leibniz's approach to notation was much
simpler. The controversy over who had invented
calculus had continued for centuries between
Society mathematicians and their counterparts on
the Continent because of nationalistic chauvinism.
While Babbage poked great fun at Newtonian
calculus, it was a very slow process to convince
professors at his own alma mater to accept his
argument and to improve their teaching by using the
Leibniz approach.

It was also at Cambridge that Babbage had his
first ideas about a calculating machine. In his
autobiography, PASSAGES FROM THE LIFE OF A

PHILOSOPHER, he reports that while staring at a
table of logarithms in the quarters of the
Analytical Society he conceived of the idea that
these tables could be calculated mechanically. He
had met his life's obsession, as one historian
noted.

Although he would eventually inherit and
spend an inheritance from his father on his
obsession, young Babbage first turned to
governmental grants to finance his initial forays
into developing his device which he called the
Difference Engine. Powered by a steam engine, the
gadget raised weights which were used to turn gears
that assisted in the computation of the constant
order of differences, a table of logarithms.

Seeking funds to build the Difference Engine,
Babbage put forward a proposal to the prestigious
Royal Astronomical Society of London. They endorsed
the concept and persuaded the chancellor of the
exchequer to grant 1500 pounds to the inventor for
research and development. This was the first of the
numerous governmental grants awarded to computer
related projects. Unlike most other governmental
grants in this area, this one was doomed to failure
from the start.

The Difference Engine that Babbage conceived
of never became a reality for two reasons. First,
Babbage was a perfectionist beyond reason. In fact,
he drove his engineer-toolmaker, Joseph Clement, to
desperate acts. For example, Clement confiscated
all copies of the blueprints in response to
Babbage's criticisms and unreasonable demands.
Babbage also was always revising and making the
plan more complicated. Second, the precision of the
tool industry was not sophisticated enough to
produce to Babbage's satisfaction the components
needed for the Difference Engine.

Sometime toward the end of the nineteen years
during which he worked on the Difference Engine,
Babbage concocted a grander scheme that would be,
conceptually, the forerunner of the modern
computer. Also, at one of his renowned parties, he
met a married woman who would have a profound
effect on his life. Augusta Ada, the daughter of
the poet Lord Byron, and Babbage were quite
attracted to one another. She chronicled Babbage's
revolutionary ideas for the world.

Babbage called his latest idea for a computing

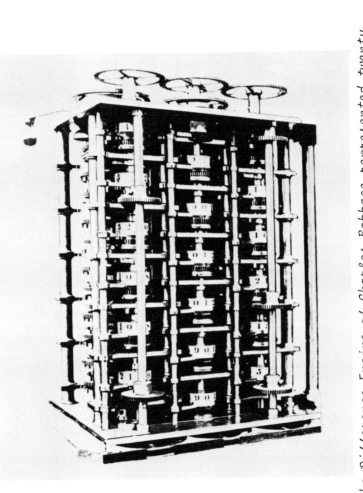

The Difference Engine of Charles Babbage represented twenty years of labor but financial difficulties prevented it from being completed. (Photo courtesy of IBM Archives)

device the Analytical Engine. In his design he
included all the components of the computer as we
know it. It included a capacity for memory, which
Babbage called "the store." Control of the
functions was to be dictated to the machine by
variable cards. Given input from the variable
cards, the Analytical Engine was designed to make
decisions. As with the Difference Engine, however,
Babbage had conceived of a marvelous idea but his
neurotic exactations would be fatal to the project
in the production phase. There is further evidence
of Babbage's neurotic tendencies. It seems he had a
developed an ongoing feud with the street musicians
of London. This hostility probably developed
towards one individual, but was generalized and
transferred to the whole group. Babbage died
October 18, 1871. His death was marked by the
street musicians of London gathering outside his
house to play. Babbage's life could be summed up as
the right person born at the wrong time. If his
life had coincided with the rapid rise of
electronic technology that began fifty years after
his death he probably would have succeeded in
making operational the computers he conceived.
Ultimately, it was the available mechanical
technology that thwarted his efforts.
     Part of the credit for the design of the
Analytic Engine belongs to Augusta Ada. While she
and Babbage always maintained a proper Victorian
appearance to their relationship, their deeply felt
love for one another was hard to conceal. Augusta,
a well respected mathematician and highly
intelligent woman, contributed to the project by
suggesting the use of punch cards. This idea was
first used by a Frenchman, Joseph-Marie Jacquard,
to control a loom. More importantly, Ada proclaimed
her lover's ideas and designs to the scientific
world through many publications. It is because of
her efforts that Babbage's creative mind and
original ideas were preserved for history. She
created her own place in the history of computers,
however, with her adaptation of the punch card to
computing processes. This idea would soon be
applied across the Atlantic to a computing device
that would show the world the labor saving
potential of the computer.
     In the late nineteenth century America was
teeming with the influx of the new immigrants. The

problem of counting the masses of new arrivals was an arduous but necessary act mandated constitutionally. The son of German immigrants, Herman Hollerith studied to be an engineer but began his work with computing devices as a result of his work as a special agent with the Census Bureau.

Working during the 1880 census, Hollerith saw firsthand the tedious and time-consuming process of tabulating, sorting, and analyzing the mountains of data collected by the census takers. He knew he could greatly simplify the process. In 1882 he became an instructor at Massachusetts Institute of Technology and taking advantage of the school's workshop he began construction of a tabulating system. Relying on a system of punched cards he fashioned a reader which consisted of a small press made up of an array of pins and an underlying bed of tiny cups of mercury. As a card was read, if the pins passed through holes, the electrical circuit was completed and simple counters were advanced automatically. Hollerith's use of electricity made his machine faster, smaller, and more reliable than mechanical machines could have ever been.

Impressed with Hollerith's work, the Census Bureau arranged for a test to prove the efficacy of his device. When compared to two other systems for counting the data, Hollerith's system proved far superior and ten times faster than the competition. He was awarded a contract for the 1890 census and it is estimated that his machine saved $5,000,000 and completed the job two years sooner than the 1880 census. Hollerith's system was adopted all over the world. The French, Austrians, Russians, and Canadians all rented Hollerith's equipment to complete their own population counts. While the rental of equipment was immensely profitable, it created a cash flow problem. The best solution seemed to be a merger, and in 1911 Hollerith's firm, the Tabulating Machine Co., joined three other companies to form what would eventually become IBM.

The efforts of the quintessential dreamer, Babbage, and the practical realist, Hollerith, are remarkable achievements in the evolution of the computer. While Hollerith's machine actually functioned and revolutionized data tabulating and record-keeping practices, it was not sophisticated

Herman Hollerith's Tabulator and Sorter Box was a computing device that revolutionized census taking. (Photo courtesy of IBM)

enough to solve complex mathematical operations such as linear equations. A machine with that type of capability required someone who could complete Babbage's design of the Analytical Engine. This effort to build a computer as we know it proceeded on two different continents by nations engaged in World War II. The Allies took advantage of the computer. If the vanquished Axis powers had capitalized on the invention of one of their own scientists, the outcome of the war might have been quite different.

THE COMPUTER DREAM BECOMES REALITY

Hating the mathematical drudgery of his engineering profession Konrad Zuse, a young German, began working on a machine that would far outstrip the capabilities of the calculator. In 1934 he began work on an electrical digital computer that brought an improved version of Babbage's dream to fruition. What is noteworthy about this advancement is that Zuse would not become aware of the Englishman's work until the outbreak of World War II and the German High Command's monumental oversight in not applying it to their scheme of world hegemony.

Using the basic rules of Boolean algebra, which are binary or able to process only two entities at a time, Zuse decided that the machine could work by using relays as digital switches. Working with a cohort who had a background in electrical engineering, Zuse and Herman Schreyer completed a prototype of a functioning computer in the living room of Zuse's parents. In 1942 he submitted a plan to the German Army High Command to produce an electronic calculator if given the necessary component parts. The High Command arrogantly denied the plan on the assumption that Germany's victory was imminent and such a machine would not have an immediate effect on that effort. Eventually, Zuse would develop an electronic calculating machine that would be used in the production of flying bombs, but at that point, Allied victory was inevitable. Unlike their adversaries, the United States had recognized the potential of computers to help end the conflict. With the collapse of Nazi Germany, Zuse's computer was relegated to the back pages of history and a

museum in Munich. The Allies, on the other hand,
were conceiving the computer as a practical way to
solve a major artillery problem.

Artillery was a major tactical element in the
military effort. Accuracy depended on ballistics
tables computed by hundreds of mathematicians
employed by the War Department. Thousands of tables
had to be computed based on the type of weapon,
size of projectile being used, and the variety of
atmospheric conditions that might exist. Compiling
these firing tables was an arduous and
time-consuming process and the United States seemed
hopelessly behind in the production of these vital
links to military success. Under sponsorship of the
National Defense Research Center, work began on an
electronic digital computer that could quickly
generate the necessary data.

The Moore School of Electrical Engineering, a
typical three-story academic structure on the
University of Pennsylvannia campus, was the
birthplace of a technological marvel that would
eventually help solve the artillery table shortage,
usher in the age of nuclear weapons, and
revolutionize the world. A proposal written by John
W. Mauchly, a thirty-five-year-old assistant
professor at the school, was initially ignored by
the War Department but eventually an agreement was
struck and Mauchly began collaborating with J.
Presper Eckert to use hundreds of vacuum tubes in
constructing an electronic computer capable of
calculating hundreds of multiplication tables per
second.

Mauchly's proposal was based on a machine that
John Atanasoff, a professor of mathematics and
physics at Iowa State University, had actually
constructed just prior to the outbreak of the war.
Called the ABC, Atanasoff's computer was limited in
two important areas, its programmability and
automaticity. Recognizing these shortcomings,
Mauchly and Eckert's modifications included
structures for including programmability and
automaticity. Unfortunately, through the
incompetence of his attorney, Atanasoff did not
legally claim a patent for his idea. With the
Japanese attack on Pearl Harbor, Atanasoff's
interest in the project waned and the machine was
disassembled by 1948. Tragically, he failed to
appreciate and take advantage of his invention.

Mauchly, who knew Atanasoff and his work, eventually took the credit with Eckert for building the first digital electronic computer. In truth, however, the pre-war inventions of Zuse and Atanasoff could both make equal claim to the same distinction. Legally, the courts have recognized Atanasoff as the rightful inventor of the automatic digital electronic computer in HONEYWELL vs. SPERRY in 1971. Historians, however, must ultimately resolve this, as there are some legal questions regarding the grounds on which the judge based his decision. Until historians convince us otherwise, most of the world will rightfully or wrongly recognize Mauchly and Eckert's ENIAC as the first computer.

The Electronic Numerical Integrator Calculator (ENIAC) was a computer that could perform the mundane calculations used in firing tables with incredible speed and unconceivable accuracy. It operated with a probability of malfunction of about 1.7 billionth of a chance of failing for any given second. ENIAC consisted of over 17,000 electronic tubes that pulsed electrical energy throughout the forty panels which included the cycling unit, accumulators, and master programmer of the unit. This sprawling mass of tubes and wires was arranged in a horseshoe shape within a large room on the ground floor of the Moore school. Ironically, the work on ENIAC wasn't completed until after the Japanese had surrendered and the war was over. It never calculated the firing tables it was designed for. Instead, ENIAC, and its descendents, played a critical role in the development of a far more powerful weapon that figured prominently in the Cold War, the hydrogen bomb.

While ENIAC was a programmable computer, the effort required to program it was considerable. It included writing detailed descriptions that defined the problem and procedure(s) for solving it. These instructions were then used to manually adjust switches and plug in hundreds of cables. It took a team of at least five highly trained workers a minimum of several days to connect the external wiring and correct whatever errors they made in the programming process. In the era of the microcomputer this is referred to as debugging.

Like Charles Babbage's progression from the

J. Presper Eckert, Jr., one of the inventors who developed ENIAC--one of the original electronic digital computers. (Photo courtesy of IBM Archives)

Difference to the Analytical Engine a century
earlier, Mauchly and Eckert began working on the
Electronic Discrete Variable Computer (EDVAC)
before work on its predecessor ENIAC had been
completed. A new member of the Eckert and Mauchly
team was John Von Neumann, a brilliant
mathematician, who helped them and the other
engineers who worked under the contract with Army
Ordnance to develop EDVAC to refine their ideas.
This was important as Von Neumann's participation
served to mitigate the impact of criticism directed
at the project. Howard Aiken from Harvard and
George Stibitz at Bell Laboratories, both respected
pioneers in the computer's development, were vocal
critics of the EDVAC team's efforts. To counter
this, Von Neumann wrote a masterful analysis and
coherent description of a computer that contains
all the features that are readily recognized as the
essentials of a computer. Each of these elements, a
central processor, ROMS, RAMS, bits, and program
storage, will be described in some detail in the
next chapter.

By the Spring of 1946 signs of a storm were
brewing among members of the EDVAC team. The
dispute centered on who owned the patent to EDVAC.
It was a three-cornered affair with Eckert and
Mauchly, the University of Pennsylvania, and Von
Neumann all laying claim. By 1947 the Ordnance
Department's attorneys settled the issue and ruled
that the idea of the store program computer legally
belonged to the University of Pennsylvania's Moore
School. The work on EDVAC ground to a halt as
Eckert and Mauchly resigned their academic
positions and Von Neumann terminated his consulting
contract. EDVAC finally became a reality in 1952
under the full control of the university. Lest we
lose a global perspective on the history of
computers, it should be pointed out that the first
stored-program computer would actually become
operational across the Atlantic in Babbage's
homeland.

Alan Turing, a Cambridge mathematician and
long-distance runner of some note, joined the
Manchester University project and helped create the
Mark I. It executed its first program in 1948, four
years before EDVAC was completed. In fairness it
should be pointed out that this machine, and other
British computer projects that were simultaneously

The Harvard Mark I, one of the first computers. (Photo courtesy of IBM Archives)

under way, included basic design ideas gleaned from reading Von Neumann's report on EDVAC. Since the breakup of the Moore school team, Von Neumann had been working for the Institute of Advanced Study on a computer based on his thinking in the EDVAC effort.

Eckert and Mauchly, in the meantime, pursued the development of computers in a private enterprise. Like Hollerith, Mauchly and Eckert were granted a federal contract for research and development based on a recommendation of the Census Bureau. They proposed a marvelous computing system called UNIVAC, which was an acronym for Universal Automatic Computer. UNIVAC not only attracted government funding, the Prudential Insurance Company and A.C. Nielsen Company, the market research specialists, also backed the project and ordered models. Underestimating their costs to deliver the computer orders, and sidetracked by another computer project intended to help guide aircraft, Eckert and Mauchly eventually sold the rights to UNIVAC to Remington Rand Corp. By 1952 Remington Rand had convinced CBS of the efficacy of using UNIVAC to predict elections results. This event in history marks the rapid takeoff of the computer age.

In the next chapter the technological advancements that made the reduction of the early computers, massive machines which filled rooms in places like the Moore School, will be explained. This brief look at the rapid spread of microcomputer technology will lead into a tour of the microcomputer and an explanation of its parts and their functions. Competent social studies teachers should have a working familiarity with the parts of a microcomputer and how they function, so they can be at least as well informed as their students who are acquiring this information from a variety of sources, both as part of the school's curriculum and as a result of their own investigations.

BIBLIOGRAPHY

Augarten, Stan. BIT BY BIT: AN ILLUSTRATED HISTORY
OF COMPUTERS. New York: Ticknor & Fields, 1984.

Austrian, Geoffrey D. HERMAN HOLLERITH: FORGOTTEN
GIANT OF INFORMATION PROCESSING. New York:
Columbia, 1982.

Babbage, Charles. PASSAGES FROM THE LIFE OF A
PHILOSOPHER. London, 1864. Reprint, New York:
Augustus M. Kelley, 1969.

Baxandall, D. CALCULATING MACHINES AND INSTRUMENTS.
Revised by Jane Pugh. London: Science Museum, 1975.

Bell, Eric Temple. MEN OF MATHEMATICS. New York:
Simon & Schuster, 1937.

Bello, Francis. "The War of the Computers." FORTUNE
60 (October 1959): 128.

Bernstein, Jeremy. THE ANALYTIC ENGINE. New York:
Random House, 1963.

Boehm, George A. "The Next Generation of
Computers." FORTUNE 60 (March 1959): 132.

Braun, Ernest, and Stuart Macdonald. REVOLUTION IN
MINIATURE: THE HISTORY AND IMPACT OF SEMICONDUCTOR
ELECTRONICS. 2nd ed. Cambridge: Cambridge
University Press, 1982

Brainerd, John G. "Genesis of the ENIAC."
TECHNOLOGY AND CULTURE 17 (July 1976): 482-488.

Burck, Gilbert. "'On Line' in 'Real Time.'" FORTUNE
69 (April 1964): 141.

Bush, Vannevar. PIECES OF THE ACTION. New York:
Random House, 1963.

Cajori, Florian. A HISTORY OF MATHEMATICS. New York: Macmillan, 1919.

Davis, Nuel Pharr. LAWRENCE AND OPPENHEIMER. New York: Simon & Schuster, 1968.

Desmonde, William H., and Klaus J. Berkling "The Zuse Z3: German Predecessor of the Mark I." DATAMATION 9 (September 1966): 30-31.

Evans, Christopher. THE MICRO MILLENNIUM. New York: Viking, 1979.

Eves, Howard. AN INTRODUCTION TO THE HISTORY OF MATHEMATICS. New York: Holt, Rinehart and Winston, 1964.

Fishman, Katherine Davis. THE COMPUTER ESTABLISHMENT. New York: McGraw-Hill, 1981.

Forester, Tom, ed. THE MICROELECTRONICS REVOLUTION: THE COMPLETE GUIDE TO THE NEW TECHNOLOGIES AND ITS IMPACT ON SOCIETY. Cambridge, Mass.: MIT Press, 1981.

Freiberger, Paul, and Michael Swaine. FIRE IN THE VALLEY: THE MAKING OF THE PERSONAL COMPUTER. Berkeley, Calif.: Osborne/McGraw-Hill, 1984.

Gardner, Martin. LOGIC MACHINES AND DIAGRAMS. New York: McGraw-Hill, 1958.

Gardner, W. David. "Will the Inventor of the First Digital Computer Please Stand Up?" DATAMATION 20 (February 1974): 84-90.

Glaisher, James Whitbread Lee. "Napier, John." ENCYCLOPAEDIA BRITANNICA 11th ed. pp. 171-175.

Goldstine, H.H. THE COMPUTER FROM PASCAL TO VON NEUMANN. Princeton, N.J.: Princeton University Press, 1972.

Greenwald, John. "D-Day for the Home Computer." TIME 7 (Novemeber 1983): 76.

Hansen, Dirk. THE NEW ALCHEMISTS. Boston: Little, Brown, 1983.

Heims, Steve J. JOHN VAN NEUMANN AND NORBERT WEINER: FROM MATHEMATICS TO THE TECHNOLOGIES OF LIFE AND DEATH. Cambridge, Mass.: MIT Press, 1980.

Hodges, Andrew. ALAN TURNING: THE ENIGMA. New York: Simon and Schuster, 1983.

Hofmann, Joseph E. LEIBNIZ IN PARIS 1672-1676: HIS GROWTH TO MATHEMATICAL MATURITY. Cambridge: Cambridge University Press, 1974.

Horsburgh, Ellice Martin, ed. MODERN INSTRUMENTS AND METHODS OF CALCULATIONS: A HANDBOOK OF THE NAPIER TERCENTENARY CELEBRATION EXHIBITION. London: G. Bell and Sons, 1914.

Hyman, Anthony. CHARLES BABBAGE: PIONEER OF THE COMPUTER. Princeton, N.J.: Princeton University Press, 1983.

Kemeny, John. MAN AND THE COMPUTER. New York: Charles Scribner's Sons, 1972.

Lavington, Simon. EARLY BRITISH COMPUTERS. Bedford, Mass.: Digital Press, 1980.

Loveday, Evelyn. "George Stibitz and the Bell Labs Relay Computers." DATAMATION 23 (September 1977): 80-85.

Lukoff, Herman. FROM DITS TO BITS: A PERSONAL HISTORY OF THE ELECTRONIC COMPUTER. Portland, Ore.: Robotics Press, 1979.

Malik, Rex. AND TOMORROW THE WORLD? INSIDE IBM. London: Millington, Ltd., 1975.

Margerison, T.A. "Computers." A HISTORY OF TECHNOLOGY. Edited by Trevor I. Williams. Oxford: Clarendon Press, 1978. pp.1150-1203.

Mauchly, John W. "Amending the ENIAC Story." DATAMATION 25 (October 1979): 217-219.

McCorduck, Pamela. THE MACHINE WHO THINKS. San Francisco: W.H. Freeman & Co., 1979.

Metropolis, N., and J. Worlton. "A Trilogy of Errors in the History of Computing." ANNALS 2 (January 1980): 49-59.

Metropolis, N.; J. Howlett; and Gian-Carlo Rota, eds. A HISTORY OF COMPUTING IN THE TWENTIETH CENTURY. New York: Academic Press, 1980.

Morrison, Philip, and Emily Morrison, eds. CHARLES BABBAGE AND HIS CALCULATING ENGINES. New York: Dover Publications, 1961.

Pullman, J.M. THE HISTORY OF THE ABACUS. New York: Praeger, 1969.

Randell, Brian, ed. THE ORIGINS OF DIGITAL COMPUTERS. New York: Springer-Verlag, 1982.

Rosen, Saul. "Programming Systems and Languages: A Historical Survey." PROCEEDINGS OF THE SPRING JOINT COMPUTING CONFERENCE, 1964 pp.1-16.

Sammet, Jean E. PROGRAMMING: HISTORY AND FUNDAMENTALS. Englewood Cliffs, N.J.: Prentice-Hall, 1969.

Shurkin, Joel. ENGINES OF THE MIND: A HISTORY OF THE COMPUTER. New York: W.W. Norton, 1984.

Smith, David Eugene. HISTORY OF MATHEMATICS. 2 vols. New York: Dover Publications, 1958.

Smith, David Eugene, ed. A SOURCE BOOK IN MATHEMATICS. New York: McGraw-Hill, 1929.

Steinmann, Jean. PASCAL. New York: Harcourt, Brace & World, 1962.

Turck, Joseph A. ORIGINS OF MODERN CALCULATING MACHINES. 1921. Reprint, New York: Arno Press, 1972.

Venn, John. "Boole, George." DICTIONARY OF NATIONAL BIOGRAPHY pp. 369-370.

Williams, M.R. "The Difference Engines." THE COMPUTER JOURNAL 19 (February 1976): 82-89.

Williams, M.R. "From Napier to Lucas: The Use of Napier's Bones in Calculating Instruments." ANNALS 5 (July 1983): 279-296.

Wulforst, Harry. BREAKTHROUGH TO THE COMPUTER AGE. New York: Charles Scribner's Sons, 1982.

CHAPTER 2

THE MICROCOMPUTER REVOLUTION:

SMALL IS BEAUTIFUL

This chapter will trace the rapid rise of the
computer as a mainstay of technology in the
information age. It will include looking at the
development of microelectronic technology, in the
form of transistors and silicon chips, as well as
languages used to program computers. The various
generations of computers will be traced up to the
microcomputer. The focus of the chapter will then
shift to describing the component parts, and the
interaction of these parts in a microcomputer
system.

ADVANCES IN MICROTECHNOLOGY

A discovery in electrical engineering that was
pivotal in the rapid advancement of the computer
after ENIAC, EDVAC, Mark I, and other models of
first-generation computers were put together, can
fit in the palm of your hand. This miniature device
had origins at about the same time as electronic
digital computers were becoming a reality in the
late 1940's and early 1950's, although both would
develop along paths that would not intersect until
the 1970's. This remarkable discovery could amplify
electronic current, as well as act like a switch
and detect radio current. It had many advantages
over vacuum tubes. For instance, it was much
smaller, generated little heat, was very
inexpensive, and was remarkably reliable. This
simple device, which would revolutionize the
electronics industry and the world, is the
transistor.

Scientists had considered semiconductors,
which is another way of describing what a
transistor does, for several decades. They were
baffled by the behavior of semiconductors and
frustrated with the fact that a transistor's
electrical current was easily affected by

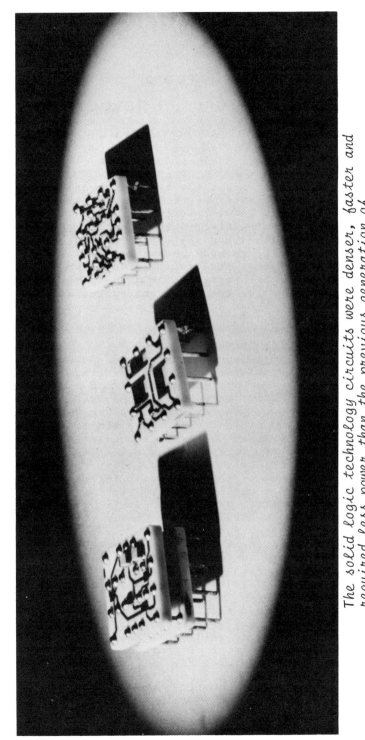

The solid logic technology circuits were denser, faster and required less power than the previous generation of transistor technology. (Photo courtesy of IBM)

contamination during its production. With the
shortcomings of radar becoming evident in World War
II, scientists began serious study for a way to use
one of two substances, silicon and germanium, which
were not so susceptible to contamination. By 1952 a
Bell Lab team of physicists, headed by the
brilliant William Shockley, had developed the
point-contact transistor. This miniscule item,
which could conduct electrical current in a much
more efficient way than a vacuum tube, naturally
attracted the attention of computer manufacturers.
They were interested because the state of the art
computers at this point required a massive facility
to house the tens of thousands of tubes. They knew
that computing would not be practical until it was
done on a smaller scale.

As the second generation of computers, which
used transistors instead of vacuum tubes, were
rolling off the production lines, a second
breakthrough in electrical circuitry occurred. An
English engineer, William Dummer, began developing
an integrated circuit, which we more commonly refer
to as the silicon chip. Physically, the silicon
chip looks like a thin wafer. It is about a 1/4 of
an inch in size. An integrated circuit is a single
solid circuit consisting of many transistors. This
arrangement greatly reduces the number of
components and interconnections. Unfortunately,
Dummer was unable to manufacture an integrated
circuit that actually worked. He suffered the same
fate as other British inventors, Charles Babbage
for instance, who were long on ideas, but short on
working models. The government declined to fund the
project beyond its early developmental stages.

As has been the case throughout the history of
the computer, the United States Army saw the value
of the integrated circuit and agreed to fund the
project to build one. This investment in another
computer-related research and development project
was justified by the Army on the basis that
advances in microelectronics served to maintain
United States superiority in the Cold War arms
race. By 1958 Jack Kilby, an engineer at Texas
Instruments, had produced a functional integrated
circuit. Because of its immense potential, there
ensued intense commercial interest in the patenting
and production of integrated chips. This highly
competitive market would eventually find a home in

Transistors and other electrical elements have been combined to form a circuit card. (Photo courtesy of IBM)

what we now call the Silicon Valley just south of
San Francisco. Most people began using silicon chip
technology when they started operating handheld
calculators.

LEARNING TO COMMUNICATE WITH THE NEXT TWO GENERATIONS OF COMPUTERS

During the same period of time as the discovery
of transistors and integrated circuits, there were
other important developments in the computer
industry. For example, several programming
languages were created. Alan Turing, the British
mathematician who was one of the early pioneers in
developing electronic digital computers, developed
an assembly language. A programming language, COBOL
(COmmon Business-Orientated Language) was developed
by a woman officer in the Navy, Grace Murray
Hopper. A team of programmers at IBM created
FORTRAN (FORmula TRANslation). Programmers refer to
COBOL, FORTRAN, and PASCAL as compilers. A compiler
translates one's program into machine code or a
binary mathematical representation system which the
machine reads as changes in voltage levels.
Computers can only understand machine code. In
addition to compiler type languages, another way of
translating a program into machine code is the
popular language BASIC (Beginner's All-purpose
Symbolic Instruction Code). The difference between
these languages is that compiler languages actually
translate a program into machine code which is
permanently saved on a disk. On the other hand,
interpreter languages translate each instruction in
a program into machine code each time the program
runs. The advantage of compiler programs is their
speed. An interpreter program, however, is easier
to modify when mistakes are noted. (This is
referred to as "debugging" in programming jargon.)
The choice of languages depends on a programmer's
needs and ability to master the commands of the
language.
A parallel development to the invention of the
transistor, integrated circuits, and computing
languages was the evolution of the computer. The
first two generations of computers are referred to
as mainframes. These were the large but versatile
machines that companies like IBM and Remington Rand
marketed to those institutions and businesses that

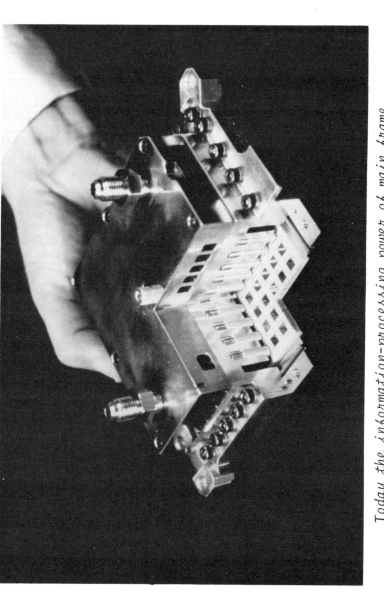

Today the information-processing power of main frame electronic computers can be held in one hand. (Photo courtesy of IBM)

were able to afford and house them. Mainframes are
now used, e.g., for complicated tasks in large
research projects which generate great numbers of
statistics.

The first minicomputer was developed by
Digital Equipment Corporation. It was about the
size of a refrigerator, relatively inexpensive, but
rather limited and slow in comparison to a large
mainframe. Nonetheless, the computer spread even
further into the fabric of our society. It was now
becoming commonplace in banks, engineers' offices,
and even submarines of the U.S. Navy. The computer
industry flourished as a result and Digital
Corporation faced a stiff challenge from many
computer manufacturing firms.

The microelectronic industry was running into
difficulty keeping up with the demand for chips.
The chips were not interchangeable; one chip
designed for one device could not be used in
another piece of equipment. A breakthrough solution
to the problem was the result of the efforts of a
young electrical engineer, Marcian Hoff, who worked
at Intel, the largest manufacturer of integrated
circuits. Hoff devised a microprocessing chip that
could be programmed as either ROM or RAM chips.
(The particular functions of ROMs and RAMs will be
described shortly.) The significant fact is that
microprocessing chips eliminated the need for logic
chips and drastically reduced the size of a
programmable computer. More importantly, the
microprocessing chip ushered in the age of the
personal computer.

A personal computer could have been
constructed as early as 1970. Several companies,
including Digital, toyed with the idea but
abandoned it because they did not believe the
personal computer, which is another name for a
microcomputer, would be marketable. A couple of
years later, articles began appearing in popular
electronics journals describing how a personal
computer could be designed in one's own workshop.
These articles attracted a great deal of attention
and the potential of a market for personal
computers began to grow.

Two young Californians saw that opportunity
and turned it into an embodiment of the Horatio
Alger story. Steven Wozniak was a college dropout
who showed a remarkable aptitude for computer

engineering. He became a friend of a high school
electronic hobbyist, Steven Jobs. Together they
develop a microcomputer. Unable to find a buyer,
they formed a partnership, the Apple Computer
Company. One of the most successful enterprises of
the late twentieth century, Apple Computer, and
other manufacturers like Radio Shack (TRS 80 model
of microcomputers) and Commodore began to produce a
computer that was durable and inexpensive enough to
be purchased by millions of home enthusiasts and
schools. Before describing how microcomputers can
be incorporated into social studies instruction,
the remainder of this chapter will explain the
various parts of a microcomputer and how they
interact as a system. We will begin by describing
binary math which is the way all computers process
all instructions and information.

THE COMPUTER'S PROCESS FOR STORING INFORMATION

Leibniz, the early pioneer in the science of
computing, attached a religious significance to the
binary system of enumeration. He considered it as a
natural proof of the existence of God. Binary math
is part of the process a computer uses to handle
information. Binary numeration involves only two
values, 0 and 1. Most microcomputers have a
capacity for storing tens of thousands, and in some
cases hundreds of thousands, of cells of
information. This information, or data, can be of
two types. Numeric data refers to numbers. Alpha
data refers to letters of our alphabet. In either
case, the data are stored for the computer in eight
"high-low" switches, which measure voltage levels.
Each voltatge level, known as a bit, is high if it
is a one. Obviously, the bit is in the low mode if it is
a zero. The fact that the voltage levels are
arranged in a group of eight (known as a byte) is
significant because each byte occupies an address
in the computer's memory. Some machines, thought
not the ones typically found in schools, can have
bits in multiples of eight. Often a computer's
memory is described as having so many K. This
simply refers to the number of thousands of
individual cells of memory, or bytes. Thus, a
machine with 64K has a capacity for sixty-four
thousand bytes of memory.
As was explained above, the bit records

information either high or low voltage depending on
whether the code was 1 or 0. Given eight bits to
the byte, each cell of information is capable of
being coded in 256 ways if you work out all the
permutations and combinations. Thus, all the
letters of the alphabet and graphic symbols such
as the asterisk can be stored. Of course, a bit
could also recode numbers from the decimal system.
For example, the decimal 2 is 10 in binary; 3 is
11; 4 is 100; 5 is 101; 6 is 110; 7 is 111. A piece
of alpha datum, such as Q could be coded 01010001.
Again, each byte is a cell of information stored in
eight, or a multiple of eight, voltage levels which
only recognize the binary values 0 and 1. The
number of cells of information, or addresses in the
computer's memory, is described as K. Sixty-four K
means that there are sixty-four thousand bytes of
memory, or possible addresses, where the
information in a set of eight high low voltage
levels can be stored.

A FANTASY JOURNEY INSIDE AND AROUND A COMPUTER

     One activity that the social studies teacher
can use to help students learn about the parts and
functions of a microcomputer is to use an
educational technique known as a fantasy journey or
a cognitive guided imagery session (DeVoe and
Render, 1982). The purpose of this activity is to
teach students how to relax their bodies in order
to better use their mental abilities of
visualization. Relaxation is achieved by a deep
breathing exercise that also alternately tenses and
relaxes muscle groups systematically.
     Cognitive guided imagery represents a unique
use of human consciousness that can be a rich
source of learning for students of all ages since
over ten percent of the human brain is involved as
it visualizes information as an input for
memorization. The following activity can be used by
both elementary and secondary teachers to help
their students learn about the inner parts of a
microcomputer and how they work. In addition to
explaining the process of a fantasy journey, the
following description should also help you get a
better picture of a how a microcomputer works.
     If you are not familiar with a deep breathing
and systematic muscle relaxation technique, begin

by teaching your students the relaxation sequence
described by DeVoe and Render (1982). It is
probably advantageous to teach this activity to
your students a few times before you actually
attempt the fantasy journey. With some practice,
the students will become comfortable with the
relaxation sequence and will be able to apply their
visualization abilities. Remind the students to
keep their eyes closed so they can concentrate on
their mental picture. When you think they are
sufficiently relaxed, take them on the following
journey using a soft, quiet, and relaxed voice.

Imagine yourself playing a stereo
record. As you play a record, there are
several parts of the system that are all
working at the same time. The music, or
data, for the record player is stored on
the record disk which consists of
concentric grooves. When you put that
record on the turntable it comes into
contact with a needle that is able to
read the messages on the record and
through electrical energy is able to send
the messages through wires to the
speakers. The energy is now converted to
sound which we hear as music or whatever
data was stored on the record grooves.
A computer works in a similar way.
If you take a floppy disk from its outer
envelope you will see that it is round
like a stereo record, but a floppy disk
is much thinner and does not have
concentric circles. Just as you would
handle a record very carefully, you want
to handle the disk so as not to damage
it. For example, you would never touch
the disk, except by the protective inner
sleeve. Just as you would never leave a
record in the hot sun because it would
warp, a floppy disk should not be exposed
to extreme heat. Another way you could
damage the information on a floppy disk
is by putting it too close to a magnet or
an electromagnet like a television. The
data on a record, on the other hand, is
actually etched onto the surface, and
placing it near a magnetic field will not

he Fantasy Journey, a teaching strategy using cognitive
magery, is an excellent way to introduce the operation of a
omputer.

affect it. Careful handling will mean a longer lifespan for both the computer disk and record.

To have the computer read the data, imagine yourself inserting the disk, with the slot in the inner envelope toward the back, into a disk drive. The disk drive acts like a record needle and converts the information on the disc, which is stored by an electromagnetic process, into an electrical impulse. Imagine yourself traveling as a jolt of electricity very quickly through the wires and into the heart of the microcomputer, the central processing unit (CPU). It is here that the information that was once contained on the disk is routed to a microprocessing chip. There are different models, or names, for these chips and depending on the brand of computer you could encounter a 8008, a 6800, or a Z80A. Whatever model of microprocessing chip, it will serve the CPU by holding information. It is here, in a single cell of memory on a microprocessing chip, that you as the electrical impulse will be processed by the CPU. Upon arriving at a memory cell, the impulse is interpreted as eight high or low voltage levels in a memory cell. It is through these voltage level interpretations that a computer sends electrical current and can process the data that has been sent.

Having set the eight bits, which constitute a byte of memory, picture yourself as an electrical impulse being combined with the information contained in the other cells of the computer's memory. At an orderly rate and with incredible speed, the computer sends you, and the other electrical impulses, to an input/output (I/O) device. In this case, it is a video-screen (CRT). You are now the message that began as magnetic code and became an electrical impulse. You have been sent from the disk drive to the eight switches of a cell of memory on a

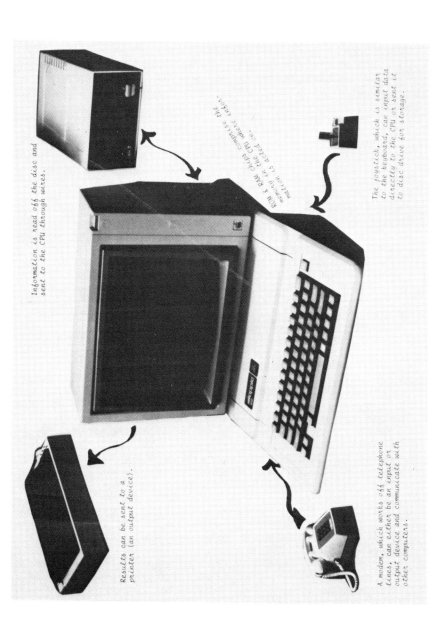

Information is read off the disc and sent to the CPU through wires.

ROM & RAM & the computer comprise the memory in the CPU where the data is acted on.

The joystick, which is similar to the keyboard, can input data directly to the CPU or sent it to disc drive for storage.

Results can be sent to a printer (an output device).

A modem, which works off telephone lines, can either be an input or output device and communicate with other computers.

microprocessing chip. From there you were
sent with other electronic signals to the
CRT. What kind of message are you? You
could be a mathematical problem; part of
a word in a story; or, a line in a
graphic. What message or picture have you
and the other electrical signals become?

After the teacher has led the students on a
fantasy journey through the inner-workings of the
computer, the students will be in a better position
to understand the various components of a
microcomputer and how they operate as a system. The
following discussion provides the necessary
background information the social studies teacher
would need to explain what the parts of a computer
are, and how they operate as a system. The diagram
on the next page is a visual overview of the
computer's four parts.

DEVICES FOR STORING DATA

As has been explained, the data stored on a
floppy disk are the chief way people communicate
with a computer. The disk drive, which is often
called peripheral storage, is a place where data
can be either sent or retrieved by the CPU. The
disk drive analyzes the magnetically stored
information on the disk and changes it to
electrical impulses that are sent back to the
computer's central processing unit. The data or
programs are arranged into parallel, concentric
tracks on the disc. Each track is divided into
sectors. The standard is 16 sectors per track.
Depending on the type of disk drive being used, a
floppy disk can have anywhere from 22 to 40 tracks.
Disks for microcomputers come in three sizes: 3 1/2
inch, 5 1/4 inch, and 8 inch. Most disks
encountered in schools are 5 1/4-inch but these can
hold a great amount of information. In fact,
several chapters of a book can be stored on a
single disk.
Floppy disks are either single or double sided,
the latter meaning the manufacturer certifies that
data can be encoded on both sides. In order to do
this, the disk must have a small notch on opposite
sides that is used by the disk drive in its search
for the sector(s) and track(s) where a requested

program may reside. This can be done by the user with the careful use of an ordinary hole punch. This procedure must be used judiciously, however. Improper placement of the notch will result in a damaged disk and lost data. For valuable programs, the reader is advised to use just one side of a disk to store programs if it is a single sided disk.

Both single and double sided disks can be single or double density. Density refers to the amount of information that can be stored on a side. Obvioulsy, a double density disk can hold twice as much information.

There are two ways to activate a disk drive. With most computers, just turning on the equipment is a signal for the CPU to start communicating with the disk drive. Any floppy disk that has been inserted into the drive automatically sends its data, called a software program(s) or file(s), to the CPU. The user can then instruct the CPU what to do with the program it has transferred to its cells of memory. Loading a disk into the drive and then turning on the machine is called cold booting a program.

A second way to activate a disk drive is called warm booting. This occurs when the machine is already on and the user wants to change disks or have the CPU erase all presently stored memory and re-enter the data on the disk. The user simply types a certain set of instructions, easily learned, or pushes certain keys. Whatever command or special keys are used, the CPU's memory is cleared and the program(s) currently on the disk will be loaded into the CPU's memory. The keyboard, an I/O device which will be discussed shortly, can also be used to send information the user has entered into the CPU to the disk to be saved for future use. For example, a user may have loaded a word processing or data base management program into the memory to either add or change the information. Once the changes have been made the user then sends the revised program back from memory to the disk in the drive where it can be saved.

In addition to floppy disks microcomputers can also use hard disks. Generically known as Winchesters because IBM first introduced a hard disk with a model number 3030 which corresponds to

FLOPPY DISK ANATOMY

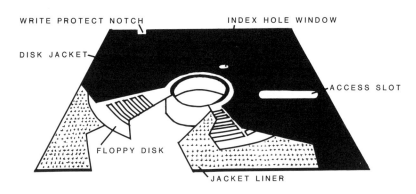

WRITE PROTECT NOTCH
INDEX HOLE WINDOW
DISK JACKET
ACCESS SLOT
FLOPPY DISK
JACKET LINER

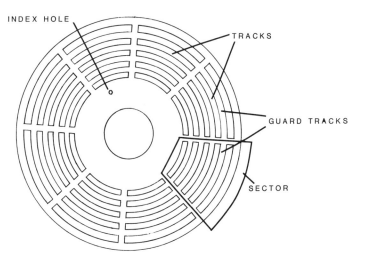

INDEX HOLE
TRACKS
GUARD TRACKS
SECTOR

the calibration of the rifle manufactured by the Winchester Company. Hard disks have several advantages and a couple of disadvantages when compared with floppy disks. One advantage is a hard disk is a sealed unit which provides it greater protection from accidental damage from environmental factors such as spilled liquids, static electricity, or tobacco smoke. Anyone of these factors could potentially have a deleterious effect on the unprotected floppy disk. The amount of information that can be stored on a hard disk is 10 to a thousand times more than a floppy disk. Finally, a hard disk is simply more reliable and faster with regard to information retrieval.

While some would argue that the hard disk is going to play a prominent role in education, there are presently two factors that are major impediments to their more widespread use in elementary and secondary classrooms. The first is the cost factor. Floppy disks are considerably less expensive. Second is the fact that it is more complicated to make a backup copy of the data stored on a hard disc. Nonetheless, there is some thought that the use of hard disks might become more prevalent as the cost declines and the quality of courseware improves (Bork, 1984).

The final peripheral storage device to be considered is the common cassette recorder and tape. Like a floppy disk, a cassette tape records information using magnetic encoding. Thus, computers in the early days were often equipped to use an ordinary cassette in place of a disk drive as a means of loading programs to and from the CPU. The transfer of information from a cassette tape to the computer is much slower than what can be accomplished through a disk drive. This fact together with the compactness of information on a disk account for the reason cassette tapes are rarely used as peripheral storage devices.

Having described how a computer can store information through several peripheral storage devices, the operation of the central processing unit will be explained in the following section. The chapter will conclude with a catalogue of the various I/O devices used in communicating with a computer.

CENTRAL PROCESSING UNIT (CPU): CHIPS AND MEMORY

The heart of a computer is its CPU. It is here
that all information must pass on its way to other
components of the system. For example, control of
the output system, to be discussed later, resides
within the integrated circuits that are part of the
CPU. The CPU serves to interpret the program
instructions. Additionally, the CPU performs the
arithmetic and logical operations such as addition,
subtraction, etc. Capable of understanding only a
small number of instructions, the computer's speed,
also controlled by the CPU, is what makes it
capable of dealing with much more complex logical
operations. The central processing unit also
receives information and instructions from another
component of the system, the computer's memory.
Memory is contained on microcomputer chips
designated as one of two types, ROM and RAM.

ROM chips have a certain amount of information
that is available to the computing system whenever
it is turned on. The information permanently stored
in ROM tells the machine to initially read the disk
operating system (DOS) which often resides on the
first track of a disc. DOS enables the CPU to
decide how to operate and in which order to proceed
with necessary routines so the software can be
used. A computing system must use DOS to operate,
but can only understand DOS that is specifically
designed for the brand(s) of equipment that make up
the system. Similarly, the computer language must
be compatible with the type of equipment being
used. This explains why software made for the TRS
80 will not operate on an Apple IIe. By tailoring
specific sections of courseware to make the program
commands and DOS compatible with the brand of
equipment being used, software publishers market
their products for most microcomputing systems
typically used in schools. In summary, the DOS is
what allows the user to interact with the computing
system by providing instructions for the CPU.

While some of the memory that the CPU uses is
in the ROM chips there are a greater number of
cells that are reserved for RAM. A cell of memory
on a RAM is an address that can temporarily store
information from a disk or is inputted by the
keyboard. It is this ability to receive information
from a piece of software or the keyboard that makes

A closeup of the new main logic board of the Apple IIe showing 31 integrated circuits including the 8-bit microprocessing chip and eight 64K RAM chips. (Photo courtesy of Apple Computers, Inc.)

a RAM different from a ROM, which cannot receive information other than what is already programmed into it. The RAM is analogous to a blackboard where information can be recorded until it is erased. With a microcomputer, erasure occurs when the computing system is turned off. The amount of memory available to a computer could be compared to the size of the blackboard. It should be pointed out that some software programs such as LOGO may have specific instructions for the computer that become part of the DOS. In these cases, however, the additional memory is sent to RAM and is processed along with the DOS permanently in ROM.

Since information that is being sent to the computer from any of the above devices is called input, it is easy to see how information sent from the computer is called output. Computers can be equipped in a variety of ways to present to the user, the information with which the computer has been dealing. We will begin with an explanation of how some input devices also serve as output devices. Several specialized output devices will then be explained. The discussion of special apparatus that permits the computer to communicate with the I/O device as a system will conclude this section.

INPUT/OUTPUT (I/O) DEVICES: COMMUNICATING WITH A COMPUTER

When a keyboard is used to communicate directly with a disk drive or with CPU it is called an I/O device. Of course, whatever is transmitted by the keyboard to the CPU must be eventually stored on a disk or otherwise it is lost when the CPU is shut off. There are other ways to input information to a computer's CPU, however. For example, on a visit to a library you might notice the librarian sending information using a light pen. A light pen can differentiate between the areas of light and shadow on a specially coded piece of tape attached to the lower corner of the book jacket. The signals picked up by the light pen are translated into binary code. Since this is the only language the computer can actually understand, the information can then be transferred from CPU to a disk drive which can save it for future use by the computer.

The light pen, an input device, can send information to a CPU by reading the areas of specially coded light and dark shadows. (Photo courtesy of Radio Shack, a division of Tandy Corporation)

Joysticks, paddles, and graphics tablets are
additional examples of I/O devices. These ways of
inputting data into a computer operate in a similar
way as the light pen. They accept mechanical
movement and code it in such a way that the
computer knows which way you have moved the stick
or pressed on the pad. These particular I/O devices
are very useful for creating graphics. Information
developed through any of these devices can be sent
to a disk drive and magnetically recorded to a disk
for peripheral storage. For more specific
instructions on using any particular type of I/O
device or disk drive it is recommended the reader
refer to the documentation that explains how to
operate the particular brand of equipment.

In addition to instruments that allow the user
to input information for the computer to operate
with, computing systems usually include an output
device that allows the user to see the information
that has been dealt with. The CRT, sometimes also
called a monitor or video screen, is one such
device that most people are already familiar. The
CRT is just like a television set except a CRT
receives its signals from the central processing
unit rather than a television station. In fact, a
television set can be used as a CRT when connected
to the CPU with the aid of an inexpensive
conversion kit. The advantage of using a CRT
designed specifically as part of a computing
system, which cannot be used for television
reception because it lacks a tuning circuit, is the
better resolution of the image displayed on the
screen.

A second common output device, which resembles
a typewriter without a keyboard, is the printer.
There are two types of printers used in schools,
each having its own advantages and disadvantages,
that can be connected to the central processing
unit and used for displaying information. One type
of printer is called a dot matrix. It works just
like a typewriter except the image is printed off a
ribbon by the arrangement of hundreds of tiny pins
into configurations which represent whatever alpha,
numeric, or graphic data are being printed. The
second type of printer that can be used as an
output device in a computing system is a daisy
wheel.

Both types of printers have attributes that

The joystick is an input device that codes mechanical movement in such a way that the computer knows which way you moved the stick. (Photo courtesy of Radio Shack, a division of Tandy Corporation)

are desirable. The dot matrix printer can reproduce
graphic images as well as numbers and letters of
the alphabet. The dot matrix printer is generally
faster than a daisy wheel. Printer speed is
measured as characters per second (CPS). The
resolution of a dot matrix image, however, is not
as good as can be obtained with the daisy wheel. In
fact, the printout produced by a daisy wheel is
often referred to as "letter quality." This is
because of the clear, crisp image that is printed
by the letters and numbers embossed on the print
wheel. As with many electric typewriters, different
print fonts are available on different wheels and
they can be readily interchanged. The type of
printer selected depends on the user's needs. If it
is primarily word processing, then the letter
quality product of a daisy wheel is warranted. If
the user wants to print graphics, an excellent way
to use the computer for social studies, then a dot
matrix printer will be needed. In either case, the
efficiency and quality of the equipment will be
reflected in its price tag. It should be noted that
most models of dot matrix printers are less
expensive than comparable daisy wheel models.
Finally, the reader should be aware that a third
type of printer for microcomputers is available. It
is called a laser jet printer, and as its name
implies it works very fast and produces excellent
copy. Unfortunately, the cost of this output device
is prohibitive for classroom use.

To this point in our discussion of I/O devices
we have grouped the various components according to
their function, either input or output. Some
devices can be incorporated into the system that
will perform both functions. A modem is an example
of such an I/O device. A modem is a specialized
piece of equipment that permits the computer to use
phone lines as a way of inputting or outputting
information. Modems are often used to help a
microcomputer communicate with other microcomputers
or mainframe computers which are capable of storing
and processing much larger amounts of data at
incredibly faster rates. A modem permits the user's
computer system to either receive or transmit
information to any other computer system that is
using a modem and has access to the same telephone
line. Modems hold great potential for use in
education. They would permit school districts to

create networks within or outside of the district's
boundaries. Modems could also be used to access an
inexpensive microcomputer to a more powerful piece
of technology, such as a minicomputer, and the user
would thus have access to more sophisticated
software. The modem and its uses will be discussed
in greater detail in Chapter 5.

The voice synthesizer represents another
special type of I/O device that could eventually
have a major impact on the world of computing.
Although still in early stages of development, the
voice synthesizer can recode human speech into the
binary system that the computer recognizes. The
computer can then perform whatever instructions it
is orally given by the user. Similarly, the voice
synthesizer can reconstruct binary code into a
rough approximation of the human voice. One current
use of voice synthesizers in school is to help the
blind and young children "read" words and symbols
that are produced by the user or are the
instructions in a program. The chief drawback of
voice synthesizers is the limited vocabulary that
can be stored in a memory. With time computer
science engineers may find a way around this
problem, and once they do the voice synthesizer may
replace the keyboard as the most popular I/O device
for communicating with peripheral storage and the
CPU.

THE COMPUTER AS A SYSTEM

The input/output features of a microcomputer
system are designed to operate together with the
CPU at a rate which appears to be simultaneous.
The I/O devices are connected to the CPU by either
parallel or serial interface cards and cables. As
their name implies, interface cards permit the CPU
to communicate with the peripheral storage and the
I/O device being used. The interface card actually
plugs into one of several slots located on the
motherboard of a CPU and then is connected to the
I/O equipment by means of cable. As you might
expect, certain products are designed specifically
to be used exclusively with either parallel or
serial interface. Some devices come with ports
designed to accommodate either type of interface.
With serial interface the data are transferred to
each bit separately until the byte is full and

By the addition of special cards that can be plugged into slots on the main logic board the amount of RAM can be significantly increased. (Photo courtesy of Apple Computer, Inc.)

another cell of memory is contacted through the
CPU. Although the parallel interface holds an edge
in the time required for an I/O to communicate with
a CPU, which sends information to each byte all in
one impulse rather than bit by bit, the difference
in overall time between the two types of interface
systems is negligible.

All of the aforementioned components of a
microcomputer system can be packaged by the
manufacturer in one of two ways. It can either be
produced so it all looks like one piece of
equipment, which usually means an internal serial
interface, or the various components can be
packaged as separate elements which require the
user to connect them. The latter arrangement
permits greater flexibility in choosing the
components and tying them together as a system. The
type of equipment used will vary depending on the
user's needs. The CRT, CPU, disk drive(s), printer,
and other I/O devices that were described are known
as hardware.

No matter how sophisticated the hardware, it
can only sit there. It is the software, or computer
programs which are stored on the floppy or hard
disk, that will give the computer a string of
instructions and other information necessary for
the CPU to perform whatever operation the software
has been designed to perform. Each disk may have
several computer programs stored on it. These
programs are arranged in files and are given
different names. Through special instructions given
the computer, the user can change or add a file,
rename it, or even delete it from the disk if it is
no longer wanted. If the user knows a computing
programming language such as BASIC or PASCAL, then
an original file can be created and stored on the
disk. Thus, the disk is a very versatile element in
a computing system.

While the cost of hardware has declined
considerably since the infancy of the
microcomputer, the time and effort required to
produce quality software has kept its cost more
stable. Because of this relative expense involved
in purchasing software, it is critical that social
studies teachers have a systematic process for
reviewing the quality of the software and
determining whether it is educationally useful.
Instruments designed for teachers to use in

evaluating software and commercial companies that
will perform the same service will be examined in
the next chapter. First, however, we will begin
with a catalogue of the various pedagogical methods
employed in the design of educational software.

BIBLIOGRAPHY

Ahl, David H. "Pascal, Ada, and Computer Literacy."
CREATIVE COMPUTING. 7 (July/August 1981): 116-123.

Albrecht, Robert; Leroy Finkel; and Gerald Brown.
BASIC 2nd Ed. New York: John Wiley and Sons, 1978.

A self-teaching text written for secondary
students. To be used as one works at a terminal,
this is a very good introduction to BASIC. The book
could be used in a classroom setting.

Anderson, R. E.,and D. L. Klassen. "A Conceptual
Framework for Developing Computer Literacy
Instruction. AEDS JOURNAL 14 (1981) 128-150.

Augarten, Stan. BIT BY BIT: AN ILLUSTRATED HISTORY
OF COMPUTERS. New York: Ticknor & Fields, 1984.

Well researched, this text provides a detailed
account of the development of the computer
industry. Specific chapters focus on IBM and the
personal computer. In addition to the narrative
this book features many excellent photographs (some
color) that highlight individuals and various
technological breakthroughs in the development of
the electronic digital computer.

Ball, Marion J. WHAT IS A COMPUTER? Boston:
Houghton-Mifflin Co., 1972.

Written before the development of the
microcomputer, this book is still an excellent
resource for teaching elementary aged students
about the various elements of a computing system.

Elegantly simple graphs depict the development of
computers, their functions, and flowcharting.

Barnard, Max. THE ESSENTIAL GUIDE TO HOME
COMPUTERS. New York: Simon & Schuster, 1980.

Beck, John J., Jr. "Computer Literacy for
Elementary and Secondary Teachers." Paper presented
at the Annual Meeting of the Texas Association for
Supervision and Curriculum Development. Houston,
Texas, November 5, 1980. (ERIC document
Reproduction Service No. ED 208 868.)

Bork, Alfred. "Computers in Education Today-and
Some Possible Futures." PHI DELTA KAPPAN 66
(December 1984): 239-243.

Berger, Melvin. COMPUTERS IN YOUR LIFE. New York:
Thomas Y. Crowell, 1981.

Bernstein, Jeremy. THE ANALYTICAL ENGINE. New York:
William Morrow & Company, 1981.

Billings, Karen, and David Moursand. ARE YOU
COMPUTER LITERATE. Beaverton, Ore.: Dilithium
Press, 1979.

A rich source of background information on a
variety of topics. The components and functions of
the parts of a computing system are explained. Also
described are the common societal applications of
the computer. This book is readable at a late
elementary or junior high school reading level.

Bitter, Gary. EXPLORING WITH COMPUTERS. New York:
Messner, 1981.

Bitter, Gary. "Creating an Effective Computer
Literacy Training Model." EDUCATIONAL COMPUTER. 74
(September/October 1982): 42.

Blumenthal, Howard. EVERYONE'S GUIDE TO PERSONAL
COMPUTERS. New York: Ballantine Books, 1983.

Describes the basic operation of a computer and
tells how to determine what type of system a

purchaser should choose. A list of software
distributors and their addresses is given. Also
includes reviews, books and magazines on computers.

Brown, Edmund G., Jr. "Computers and the Schools."
T.H.E. JOURNAL 10 (1982): 99-100.

Buchsbaum, Walter H. PERSONAL COMPUTERS HANDBOOK.
Indianapolis: Howard W. Sams & Co., 1980.

Buffington, Charles. YOUR FIRST COMPUTER: HOW TO
BUY IT AND USE IT. New York: McGraw-Hill, 1983.

An introductory guide to purchasing and operating a
microcomputer. It describes the various ways a
microcomputer can be used. Provides a detailed
description of how the various components of a
microcomputer operate. Concludes with a chapter on
the future of microcomputing.

Crowley, Thomas H. UNDERSTANDING COMPUTERS. New
York: McGraw-Hill, 1976.

Denenberg, Stewart A. "An Alternative Curriculum
for Computer Literacy Development." AEDS JOURNAL 13
(1980): 156-173.

DeVoe, M.W., and Gary F. Render. "Gestalt
Strategies for Elementary Social Studies." SOCIAL
EDUCATION 46 (May 1982): 348-352.

Diem, Richard A. "Computers in the Social Studies
Classroom." HOW TO DO IT SERIES, SERIES 2., NO. 14.
Washington D.C.: National Council for the Social
Studies, 1981.

Ditlea, Steve. SIMPLE GUIDE TO HOME COMPUTERS. New
York: A.& W. Visual Library, 1979.

A basic introduction to the microcomputer. Contains
a history of the development of microprocessors and
how they function. The process of binary arithmetic
is explained. Included are numerous black and white
photographs and line drawings to illustrate how a
microcomputer works.

Frank, Mark. DISCOVERING COMPUTERS. London: Trewin Copplestone Books, Ltd., 1981.

A colorful and comprehensive introduction to computers. While it does not focus on microcomputers, it does cover a variety of topics such as timesharing, computer networks, microprocessors, and the processing cycle. Provides brief treatment of more than forty topics.

Frates, Jeffrey, and William Moldrup. INTRODUCTION TO THE COMPUTER: AN INTEGRATIVE APPROACH. Englewood Cliffs, N.J.: Prentice-Hall, 1980.

Friel, S., and N. Roberts. "Computer Literacy Bibliography." CREATIVE COMPUTING 6 (1980): 92-97.

Galanter, Eugene. KIDS AND COMPUTERS: THE PARENTS' MICROCOMPUTER HANDBOOK. New York: Perigree Books, 1983.

The information provided in this comprehensive description is useful to social studies teachers as well as parents. Has excellent introductory chapters that highlight topics such as the parts of a computer, its history, and how to work with children when introducing them to the computer. The emphasis in this book, however, is on how to help children learn rudimentary programming and BASIC commands. Includes a glossary and an evaluation of computers in edcuation.

Gress, Ellen K.A. "A Computer-Literacy Module for the Junior High School." ARITHMETIC TEACHER 29 (1982): 46-49.

Horn, C.E., and J.L. Poirot. COMPUTER LITERACY: PROBLEM SOLVING WITH COMPUTERS. Austin, Texas: Sterling Swift Publishing Co., 1981.

A good introductory text with chapters on the history of computing, the role of computers in government, computer applications in other settings, computer and humans, and the value of information in society. Excellent exercises for review purposes are provided at the end of each chapter.

Hunter, Barbara. MY STUDENTS USE COMPUTERS: LEARNING ACTIVITIES FOR COMPUTER LITERACY COURSES. Reston, Va.: Reston Publishing Co., 1983.

Provides a well-rounded set of objectives relative to computer literacy. More importantly, a wealth of learning activities for the K-8 curriculum is included. Cover such topics as fundamentals, applications, impacts, and writing programs. An excellent resource for teachers; the comprehensive lesson plans are useful and well written.

Khambata, Adi. MICROPROCESSORS/MICROCOMPUTERS. New York: John Wiley and Sons, 1982.

Kirchner, Alice M. "One State's Approach to Computer Literacy." TECHNOLOGICAL HORIZONS IN EDUCATION 8 (1981): 43-44.

Luehrmann, Arthur. "Computer Literacy-A National Crisis and a Solution for It." BYTE 5 (July 1980): 98-102.

Milner, Stuart D. "Teaching Teachers About Computers: A Necessity for Education." PHI DELTA KAPPAN 61 (1980): 544-546.

Moursund, David. TEACHER'S GUIDE TO COMPUTERS IN THE ELEMENTARY SCHOOL. LaGrande, Ore.: International Council for Computers in Education, 1980.

Nelson, Ted. THE HOME COMPUTER REVOLUTION. South Bend, Ind.: The Distributors, 1977.

Osborne, Adam. AN INTRODUCTION TO MICROCOMPUTERS, VOLUME 0. Berkeley: Adam Osborne & Assoc., 1979.

Rochester, Jack, and John Gantz. THE NAKED COMPUTER. New York: William Morrow & Company, 1983.

Shelly, Gary B., and Thomas J. Cashman.
INTRODUCTION TO COMPUTERS AND DATA PROCESSING.
Brea, Calif.: Anaheim Publishing Company, 1980.

Shurkin, Joel. ENGINES OF THE MIND. New York: W.W.
Norton, 1984.

A history of the computer. Traces the development
of computers from the efforts of Charles Babbage
through the invention of the the first electronic
all-purpose digital machine. Concluding with a
brief   chapter on the microcomputer, the book's
primary focus is on mainframes. It is well
researched and has an extensive bibliography and
reference section.

Sipple, C.J. MICROCOMPUTER HANDBOOK. New York: Van
Nostrand Reinhold Co., 1977.

Has coverage of design and engineering topics on
microcomputers. Compares and contrasts
microcomputers with standard and minicomputers.
Describes the various types and capabilities of
microcomputers, software, programming techniques,
and the range of application.

Shockley, William. "Solid-State Circuits Used to
Build 10oz. General-Purpose Computers." AVIATION
WEEK AND SPACE TECHNOLOGY 30 (October 1961): 81.

Shockley, William. "Transistors: Growing Up Fast."
BUSINESS WEEK 5 (February 1955): 86.

Spencer, Donald D. COMPUTER DICTIONARY FOR
EVERYONE. New York: Scribner's, 1979.

Spencer, Donald D. EXPLORING THE WORLD OF
COMPUTERS. Ormond Beach, Fla.: Camelot Publishing
Co., 1982.

Waite, Mitchell, & Michael Pardee. MICROCOMPUTER
PRIMER. Indianapolis: Howard. W. Sams & Co., 1980.

A technical description of the microcomputer and
how it operates. Detailed explanations of the
electronics behind the logical operations are the

heart of this book. Includes intricate drawings and photos describing these operations. A brief introduction to programming is also provided.

Willis, Jerry. PEANUT BUTTER AND JELLY GUIDE TO COMPUTERS. Beaverton, Ore.: Dilithium Press, 1981.

Wulforst, Harry. BREAKTHROUGH TO THE COMPUTER AGE. New York: Charles Scribner's Sons, 1982.

Stimulating and readable, this account of the computer age focuses more on advancements in the twentieth century. Suitable for secondary students, it is a useful description, with a minimum of technical jargon, that should prove useful to any student interested in the history of microcomputer technology. The photographs, while not numerous, provide a graphic picture of important characters in the field.

Zaks, Rodney. DON'T: OR HOW TO CARE FOR YOUR COMPUTER. Berkeley, Claif.: Sybex, Inc., 1981.

A well-illustrated introduction to using a microcomputer. Chapters focus on individual components of a microcomputer system such as the CRT., terminal, printers, floppy disks, and include documentation. The final chapters discuss providing security for equipment, and how to obtain help when something goes wrong.

Zaks, Rodney. FROM CHIPS TO SYSTEMS: AN INTRODUCTION TO MICROPROCESSING. Berkeley, Claif.: Sybex, 1981.

CHAPTER 3

COURSEWARE AND ITS EVALUATION

Computers are wonderful tools. They are efficient, speedy, and versatile machines that hold a great deal of promise for social studies education. The key to more effective educational use is not a matter of following the trends and purchasing the latest model of computer on the market. Rather, the essential element to taking advantage of computers in social studies instruction is the selection of software. It has been estimated that only about 5% of all the educational software can be highly recommended (Komoski, 1984). Thus, it is imperative that courseware be professionally evaluated before it is recommended for purchase. Without an adequate basis for evaluation, the social studies teacher is limited in the ability to make informed choices about which software to acquire.

This chapter provides the background to enable a social studies teacher to determine evaluation strategies for choosing software directly related to social studies. In other words, software that directly teaches skills, knowledge, and values about topics related to the social studies will be considered. Often this type of software is called courseware to distinguish it from information processing software that can be enlisted for educational purposes such as teacher utility, word processing, and databases. Information processing software will be the focus of the next chapter.

A description of the various instructional strategies underlying social studies computer assisted instruction (CAI) follows. Several evaluation instruments and their particular advantages and disadvantages will be discussed. Finally, commercial software evaluation services will be identified. Because prices fluctuate so rapidly, the fee for these services will be stated as an estimated price. Exact cost of the services must be ascertained by the prospective subscriber.

By the conclusion of the chapter the reader will
not only have an appreciation for the amount of
time to devote to evaluating courseware, but also
specific strategies and models that can be utilized
in the selection of courseware. I hope that you
develop an appreciation for this critical and
complex aspect of using computers in social
studies.

INSTRUCTIONAL COMPONENTS OF COURSEWARE

The reason the computer is such an exciting
educational tool is that it adapts well to a
variety of instructional strategies. These
strategies can be employed to help students meet
different educational needs. The computer can be
used advantageously with each of these strategies
for the following reasons. First, good CAI provides
immediate feedback. It is a widely accepted
principle that learning is generally inversely
proportional to the difference in time between
response and reinforcement. The operation of a
microcomputer requires active motor and cognitive
participation by the learner. Feedback is immediate
and students can either retrace their steps or
proceed. The computer's potential for producing
dynamic graphics can perceptually organize complex
phenomena and information. Several courseware
strategies permit the breakdown of complex tasks or
material, such as map reading, into sequential
steps which can be more easily mastered. Finally,
the computer has remarkable patience. It can
provide much practice which increases the time
spent on a task, regardless of a teacher's mood or
energy level. It is the versatility and the
inherent motivational attributes of the computer
that make it so well suited to each of the four
instructional categories, drill and practice,
tutorial, simulation, and problem solving, for
which it is typically employed in social studies.

Drill and practice. The most prevalent form of
courseware encountered in social studies and most
other subject matter areas is drill and practice.
Programs of this type are often question and answer
in format and are intended for remediation and
reinforcement of one or more specific skills or
concepts. Often drill and practice courseware will
involve the learner in a game of some type. Not to

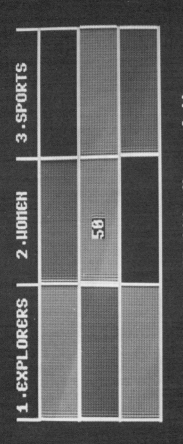

An example of a drill and practice program. (Photo courtesy of Focus Media)

be overlooked, the game dimension of drill and
practice program includes the conditions of
competition, with oneself or others, specific or
arbitrary rules, the need to develop a winning
strategy, and the introduction of random events to
force a revision of the user's winning strategy.
Based on the stimulus/response research of
psychologist B.F. Skinner, drill and practice CAI
promotes the acquisition of knowledge or a skill
through repetitive practice.

The most obvious characteristic of a drill and
practice piece of courseware is the use of paired
association for stored lists of facts. Examples of
this type of CAI strategy are the types of programs
that expect a student to match a capital to a
state, or a program that asks one to identify a
famous figure in American history after being given
three biographical facts. Not considered the most
sophisticated use of computers in education, drill
and practice remains very popular for three
reasons. First, rightly or wrongly, drill and
practice activities are essential to success in
school and teachers don't always have the time to
help all students master the material through
direct instruction. Second, student achievement
with drill and practice materials is quantifiable.
The learning objective can be clearly specified and
measured according to the number of correct
responses. Finally, drill and practice programs are
relatively easy to design and develop. Thus,
publishers of commercial software are willing to
invest capital in their production.

There is much argument about the benefits and
quality of many drill and practice programs.
Educators (Snyder & Palmer, in press) question if
this is the best use of costly computer hardware
and if drill and practice is educationally
effective. The more sophisticated drill and
practice programs employ a random presentation of
material rather than presenting it sequentially.
When material is ordered randomly, the learner is
more likely to make the memorization on the basis
of the paired association as opposed to being able
to correctly predict the ordered presentation of
the stimuli. In addition to randomization, the
better drill and practice programs make use of many
other unique capabilities of the computer.
Graphics, color, and sound can all enhance the

attractiveness of a drill and practice program.
    The simplicity of instructions and manner in
which the program operates are of paramount
importance when it comes to drill and practice. The
teacher's purpose in using this type of courseware
is to be free to work directly with other learners
while another student independently operates the
drill and practice program. The provision of
immediate feedback is another area of concern the
social studies teacher should have with regard to
drill and practice. All of the program's responses
to student answers should be positive and
encouraging. Similarly, wrong answers should be
corrected immediately, erased from the screen, and
the student should be prompted to respond again at
least once. Furthermore, an effective program will
provide a student with some suggestions to help
guide the learner's thinking. Because so much of
the available social studies courseware is drill
and practice in nature, the teacher has to be very
judicious in selecting software employing this
strategy.
    Tutorial. One of the most exciting areas in
courseware development is a situation where the
teacher/designer of the program is able to create a
dialogue with the learner using the computer as a
means of communication. The direction and level of
dialogue is dependent on the student's input. This
strategy is known as a tutorial and it is
particularly effective in engaging the learner in
activities and material that are brand new. An
effective tutorial, commonly called a dialogue,
leads the active learner through a series of
carefully planned questions which results in some
new understanding or knowledge about the topic
under study. Tutorials have been employed in CAI
since its early days when they were almost
synonymous with programmed instruction. Early
tutorials presented a frame of information, asked a
question, and then selected the subsequent
information based on the student's response. These
initial efforts at CAI were often hastily
developed, with little thought given to programs
that incorporate good teaching practices.
Fortunately, the quality and value of these
programs have increased as designers gain more
expertise and sophistication in the tutorials they
develop. As a result of this, more quality tutorial

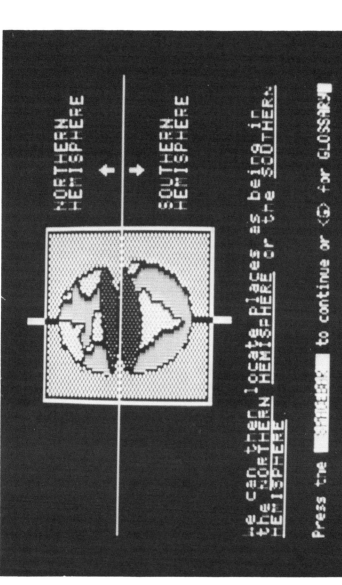

An example of a tutorial program. (Photo courtesy of Focus Media)

courseware is rapidly appearing on the market.

A good tutorial can be a real benefit to social studies teachers in rural schools or small urban schools where the limited staff is not able to offer as wide a variety of courses as they might like. For disciplines such as anthropology and economics, there may not be a qualified faculty member to serve as an instructor. Shortages in staff can be compounded if there is not a sufficient number of students who are willing to enroll in a section. Tutorials can be an excellent way to meet the needs of those who would be interested in special courses. In the elementary grades, tutorial programs have the potential to present advanced material for the highly motivated and gifted student. Tutorials could be a viable option for the homebound student or one who must be out of the classroom for an extended period of time. The use of a microcomputer and appropriate tutorial programs provide students with an independent and exciting avenue for acquiring information and developing skills that might otherwise not be learned.

When first developed tutorials were characterized as nothing more than "electronic page turning" devices. Frame after frame of information were presented but little or no interaction with the student was required. Thus, the capabilities of the microcomputer were not being used and the student was just as well off using a text or other source of information. Today careful design of a tutorial includes frequent interaction with the student. One example of this is the use of a menu which often precedes a segment or module of a tutorial and gives the learner an overview of the lesson. A menu helps the student cognizably organize new material, thus increasing the likelihood of retention.

There are additional design factors that should be taken into account when examining courseware that employs a tutorial approach. First, the sequential arrangement of material into separate modules should approximate the attention span of most learners, fifteen or twenty minutes' worth of work at a sitting. Learning objectives should be clearly defined and easily measured. The information should be arranged in an attractive and interesting fashion that best conveys its meaning.

This may include the use of graphics to accommodate
visual channels of learning. As with drill and
practice courseware, positive feedback, presented
with variety and imagination, should occur
frequently. The frequent use of tests for formative
evaluation helps the learner keep pace and take
advantage of a tutorial's branching characteristic.

In a program employing branching, a student's
response to an objective question will trigger an
appropriate response from the computer either to
proceed with material or have the student perform
additional work with previous material from the
tutorial. For example, depending on a student's
responses, a tutorial that teaches about the
economic reasons for the American Revolution might
keep the learner engaged in material on protective
tariffs before presenting any more material on
mercantilism. Perhaps the most critical factor in
the design of an effective tutorial is its ability
to judge student input and make appropriate
branching decisions. A wrong judgment will send a
student down a side path resulting in frustration
and little learning. Obviously, the more
complicated an expected response, the greater the
difficulty of having the computer make a judicious
assessment of the correctness or incorrectness of a
student's response. This explains why most
tutorials test frequently and use multiple choice,
matching, or questions to be answered by true or
false.

Many textbook publishing companies are
producing courseware to accompany the text that has
been adopted for classroom use. When a tutorial is
correlated carefully with the curriculum it can be
very effective. This means, however, that the
material must be presented in an interesting manner
that goes beyond simply transferring the textbook
to the screen. It is important that in addition to
taking maximum advantage of the capacities of the
computer a good tutorial will have adequate
documentation and be self-directing and user
friendly.

Simulation. The use of simulation courseware
in the classroom offers the social studies teacher
a good opportunity to make history come alive.
Simulation is a well-recognized social studies
method in education that predates the use of
computers. The purpose of a simulation is to create

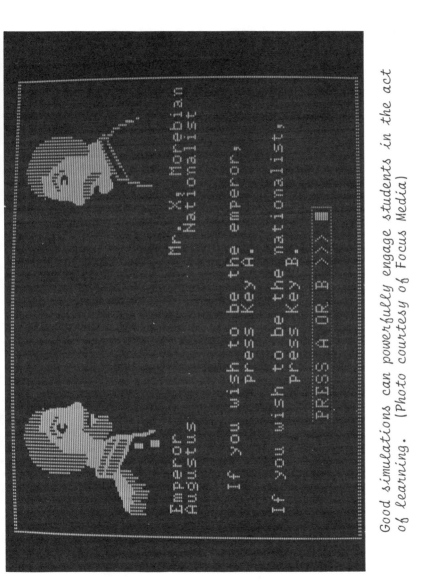

Good simulations can powerfully engage students in the act of learning. (Photo courtesy of Focus Media)

a controllable world that is very motivating to a
student because of the level of involvement
generated. Additionally, a simulation allows the
user to experience the need to make decisions
without having to suffer the dire consequences of
making a real-life wrong decision. So, too, with a
microcomputer simulation. Effective simulations
mimic a system by creating a model which involves
the learner with the behavior and interaction among
variables. This can range from replicating the
experience of running a presidential campaign to
pretending to be a tycoon trying to maintain
financial well being during the Depression. Because
microcomputers are well equipped to process a large
number of variables almost simultaneously, they are
ideal for simulations. Simulations whose outcomes
can be influenced by the user's choices offer a
good opportunity to help students gain insight and
learn decision making skills such as allocation of
financial resources or cooperation.

    One of the most common forms of simulation is
known as an adventure. In this type of simulation
students take on the role of an explorer or
fictional character and must plan strategies to
resolve situations thrust upon the character. An
adventure often requires reading comprehension
skills ranging from the fifth grade on up. A
typical adventure begins with a printed text
serving as an orientation to the simulation. This
should include a listing of the learning objectives
and the purpose behind the simulation. Game rules
and procedures for hardware use should also be
described here. After characters and other
variables affecting play are identified, the
students proceed to the decision making components
of the simulation. Usually several options for
action are available to the players and if group
consensus is arrived at, intra-group cooperation
can be fostered and reinforced. A predetermined
time limit imposed by the computer can be an
intervening factor in the decision making process.

    As with the approaches to courseware described
previously, a simulation should be easy for a
student to operate. The program should progress
quickly enough and be sufficiently motivating to
keep the student involved. The inclusion of sound
and graphics enhances the instructional quality of
the simulation. Graphics can be used in a variety

of ways including presenting information, categorizing and tabulating data, or providing feedback to the learner regarding progress. While the availability of quality social studies courseware simulations is limited, the effort and research required to locate them is well worth it. Good simulations are powerful teaching tools for a wide range of social studies objectives. It is critical when using simulations that the teacher be available to guide the students. Introductory and concluding activities, such as group discussion, should accompany CAI simulations.

Problem-solving. The ability to solve a problem is an educational goal that cuts across several disciplines. In essence, a problem-solving situation requires the learner to analyze the situation, gather relevant information, formulate a plan, test the hypothesis, and then generalize from whatever results are obtained. Problem-solving programs can intrigue students so that they begin to explore the whole world of programming as they are engaged by a problem and its possible solution(s).

Often what may be characterized on cursory inspection as only a game, actually is a sophisticated and intriguing way of engaging students in the problem-solving process described above. Problem-solving programs that appear to be games are often not content specific. In other words, the objectives of the game and the concepts being developed do not directly appear to be related to a specific discipline such as social studies. In fact, the objectives that the program teaches may be appropriate to several disciplines. In this case, the purpose is to help students learn generic skills and apply them systematically in a process.

The most sophisticated type of problem-solving courseware is the popular LOGO developed at MIT by Seymour Papert. Technically a computer programming language, LOGO was devised with the philosophy of creating an open environment where a child is free to explore the process of learning. Some speculate that LOGO gives us a glimpse of what we might expect in the next generation of educational courseware. One creative application of LOGO to the social studies classroom is to use it to create a classroom or community map. In doing so students

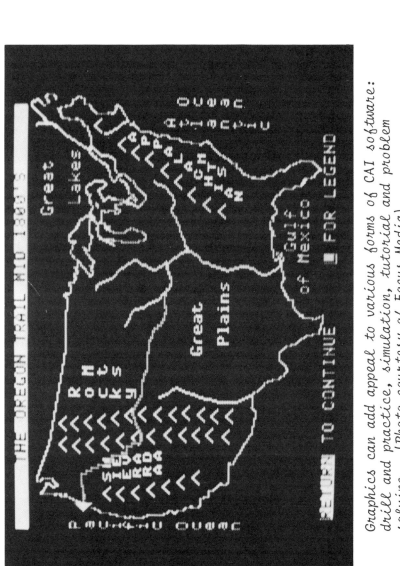

Graphics can add appeal to various forms of CAI software: drill and practice, simulation, tutorial and problem solving. (Photo courtesy of Focus Media)

DOMAINS OF COMPUTER ASSISTED INSTRUCTION

TYPES OF SOFTWARE	EXAMPLES
DRILL AND PRACTICE	AMERICAN HISTORY ADVENTURE·AMERICAN HISTORY:THE DECADES GAME· BEYOND THE RISING SUN–DISCOVERING JAPAN·LINCOLN'S DECISIONS· MEET THE PRESIDENTS
SIMULATION	AGENT USA CHOICE OR CHANCE·CARTEL AND CUTTHROATS· COMMUNITY SEARCH·CROSS COUNTRY USA·THE DISCUSSION GENERATOR:CONTEMPORARY ISSUES SERIES· ENERGY SEARCH· GEOGRAPHY SEARCH· MILLIONAIRE· THE OTHER SIDE· PRESIDENT ELECT· RAILS WEST· RUN FOR THE MONEY· SIMPOLICON·TRAIL WEST
TUTORIAL	AFRICA·THE DECISION SHOP· DEMOGRAPHICS·INTRODUCTION TO ECONOMICS· THE LANGUAGE OF MAPS (SERIES A&B)· MAP READING· POLITICAL GENIE·REVOLUTIONS:PAST PRESENT AND FUTURE·SOCIAL STUDIES VOLUME 2,6· U.S. CONSTITUTION TUTOR·UNLOCKING THE MAP CODE
PROBLEM SOLVING	ARCHEOLOGY SEARCH·JENNY OF THE PRARIE·LOGO

become absorbed in their work while they learn a
variety of mapping skills as they teach the
computer to symbolically recreate the environment
being mapped (DeLeeuw and Waters, 1985).
Problem-solving programs can range from a wide open
format, such as LOGO, to very specific problems
with clear-cut solutions.
     The social studies teacher should not overlook
problem-solving as an instructional strategy when
making decisions about courseware. Even though
problem-solving courseware may not be listed under
social studies in a publisher's directory, often it
is placed in its own separate category. The effort
to locate and evaluate problem-solving courseware
is well worth it. The game-like approach to many
problem-solving programs makes them very attractive
to students. As with simulations, the students
might be organized into groups and be developing
skills related to cooperation as well as solving
the problem presented by the program.

EVALUATING COURSEWARE: SOME BASIC CONSIDERATIONS

     Obtaining and evaluating courseware is a
responsibility that all social studies teachers
should be prepared to accept as educators in the
Information Age. Making sure that courseware being
examined for possible adoption is consistent with
the goals and the objectives of the social studies
curriculum is not to be treated lightly. Having a
systematic strategy for the evaluation process will
help the teacher meet this crucial responsibility
and ensure that courseware recommended for purchase
has been carefully selected.
     Prior to actually sitting down with a piece of
courseware and working through an evaluation
instrument, there are some basic considerations to
which the evaluator should attend. For example, the
descriptive information supplied by a vendor in an
advertising brochure should reveal the type of
computing system on which the software has been
designed to run. It should be noted that publishers
often produce several versions of a product so that
they will be compatible with leading educational
microcomputing systems. There are questions that
should be addressed before a particular piece of
courseware is requisitioned for purchase. How much

memory is required to run the program(s)? What DOS is employed? For what grade levels is the courseware designed? Can the program be obtained for review? What is the cost and accepted method of payment if a decision is made to purchase the publisher's product? Before you contact a publisher or vendor to obtain the courseware for preview, you will need this basic information regarding the compatability of the courseware with your computer system to avoid the extra expense of shipping an incompatible piece of courseware. It should be noted that some courseware producers still refuse to permit preview because they fear their software will be illegally copied and then returned to them unpurchased.

The actual evaluation process of courseware for any subject area should proceed in two steps. The first is to describe the courseware being considered in relation to the previously raised questions regarding compatibility, etc. The second is to gain specific information regarding the knowledge, skills, and values being taught in the courseware. Since the latter step will be unique to specific subject areas in the curriculum, the instrument used in this phase must be tailored to that subject area. To complete the former step, consult the general guides that describe the courseware regardless of its subject matter.

As part of the first step in the evaluation process, describing the courseware, the following six basic procedures should be followed:

1. Load the program, and become familiar with how it operates.

2. Execute the program as a top student would. Do not attempt intentional errors at this point. Mimic the behavior of a student of this type by testing the sophistication of the program.

3. Execute the program as an unsuccessful student might. How does the program respond to incorrect answers? Similarly, what happens when the user makes a typing mistake or doesn't follow directions.

4. Use an evaluation instrument that you are comfortable with and that meets your needs (See Figure 2.1). Strive for objectivity by keeping your responses on the instrument based on observations. Compare your conclusions against the claims of the publisher.

5. Evaluate the documentation and ancillary materials. The extent of this step will be contingent on the impressions you have developed as you've completed the first four steps.

6. If possible, watch several students to see how they respond to the program as they work through it. Do they seem to be learning from working with it; and if so, is it what you intend?

7. Make a decision.

Some courseware is offered in a group of from fifteen to thirty programs. A sampling technique can be employed to shorten the time for evaluating a package that otherwise could take weeks to review. The initial program in the package may reveal some conventions for easier use of the package. For example, certain commands need to be used in this initial program. Examine at least two programs that form a sequence within the package. This will help determine the interdependency of individual programs. A package of programs that are relevantly dependent on each other could create divisive administrative and classroom management issues. By testing a program near the end of the cluster, the program's upper limit can be judged. While not foolproof, this shortcut to evaluating a package of programs can save a great deal of time. The next section presents one type of courseware description instrument that can be used to complete the first step and begin the second step of the evaluation process. Also included are the guidelines for evaluating social studies courseware published by the National Council for the Social Studies. This particular document can be used for the second step of the evaluation process, assessing content. Some of the information to be

A Checklist for Evaluating the Instructional Design of Educational Software

Objective: What should the software teach your students to do?

The Question: How well and how efficiently do students who have used the program learn the skills specified above? *

1. Does the software require a high frequency of responding (as opposed to screens of material to read)? For tutorials and drills, how many problems does a student actually do in a 10-minute session?
2. Is the responding relevant to your goals? (Do students *do* what they are to learn?)
3. Do students have to respond to the critical parts of the problems?
4. Is most of the screen content necessary for the response, or does the program assume that students will learn content without having to respond overtly to it?
5. Does each screen ask students to discriminate between at least two possible responses?
6. Can students see their progress as they work with the program from day to day or session to session?
7. Are students mostly successful going through the program (as opposed to becoming frustrated)? Do they enjoy using the program?
8. For series, or lessons to be used repeatedly: Does the program adjust according to the performance level or progress of the student?

---

*The best way to judge an instructional program is, of course, to try it out with students. Even without trying a program out, however, you can usually spot programs with weak instructional design, so that you can eliminate them from those your students try.

collected in completing these documents can be
obtained from advertisements or reviews of the
courseware. This should not substitute for actually
sitting down and using the six procedures described
above. Unfortunately, sometimes vendors and
publishers cannot deliver the claims they make in
their advertisements.

COURSEWARE EVALUATION INSTRUMENTS

The National Council for the Teachers of
Mathematics (NCTM) publishes a courseware
evaluation instrument in a booklet which is
applicable to any subject area. (See Appendix A.)
The NCTM booklet contains a comprehensive
instrument and a complete description of how to use
it. The NCTM publication is easy to use and is
therefore recommended for novices. The complete
NCTM publication is titled GUIDELINES FOR
EVALUATING COMPUTERIZED INSTRUCTIONAL MATERIALS. It
can be ordered from:

> National Council of Teachers
> of Mathematics
> 1906 Reston Drive
> Reston, Virginia 22091

The National Council for the Social Studies
(NCSS) has also published guidelines for evaluating
courseware. (See Appendix A.) The NCSS guidelines
have been specifically developed for use by social
studies teachers. It is a comprehensive instrument
that focuses on the content of the program in
relation to knowledge, skills, and values of the
courseware. A disadvantage in the NCSS publication
is that it does not include a checklist for
specific details of the software in terms of
systems requirements and other
technical/instructional issues. Thus, the evaluator
must develop a technical/instructional checklist of
their own or order a technical/educational
evaluation instrument such as the NCTM instrument
above. The NCSS guidelines were originally
published in the November/December 1984 issue of
SOCIAL EDUCATION and can be reproduced without
seeking further permission from NCSS.
Also available are reviews offered by
professional services. These are usally independent

reviews which give the user an approximation of the usefulness of a given piece of software. These reviews should not, of course, be the sole basis for making a decision to purchase a piece of software. They can serve as an initial screening step and from the comments or grade given by a reviewer, a decision can be made as to whether additional review by the potential purchaser should be undertaken. The following institutions offer software reviews:

> EPPI
> Teachers College
> Columbia University
> P.O. Box 27
> New York, NY 10027
>
> MicroSift
> Northwest Eduational Regional Laboratory
> 300 SW 6th Ave.
> Portland, OR 97204
> (503) 248-6800
>
> Software Reports
> 10996 Torreyana Rd.
> P.O. Box 85007
> San Diego, CA 92138
> (619) 457-5920
>
> Digest of Software Reviews
> 301 West Mesa
> Fresno, CA 93704
> (209) 431-8300

The use of a commercial review service, or reliance on any second party review of software, should never substitute for a hands on review conducted by the potential user utilizing a systematic method such as the NCSS guidelines. This is critical to making informed choices about the educative potential of software.

BIBLIOGRAPHY

Ahl, David H. "Computer Simulation Games." TEACHER 97 (February 1980): 60-61.

The motivational power and effectiveness of simulation games on the computer are described by the author. The use of the computerized simulation as a teaching tool is described for many grades and subject areas. Social studies is briefly included.

Anderson, Ronald E. "Computer Simulation Games: Exemplars." In Robert E. Horn and Ann Cleaves, eds. THE GUIDE TO SIMULATIONS/GAMES FOR EDCUATION AND TRAINING, 4th Ed. Beverly Hills: Sage Publications Inc., 1980.

Banet, B. "Computers and Early Learning." CREATIVE COMPUTING 4 (September/October 1978): 90-95.

Becker, H.J. "Microcomputers in the Classroom: Dreams and Realities." CENTER FOR THE SOCIAL ORGANIZATION OF SCHOOLS. Report No. 319. Baltimore, Md.: The John Hopkins University, January 1982.

An in-depth look at both problems and possiblities associated with using of micromputers in the classroom. The discussion centers around instructional techniques and social aspects of integrating computer activites into ongoing classroom environments. Concludes with a summary of recommendations for researchers, developers of educational materials, and school system administrators.

Bitter, G., and R. Camuse. USING MICROCOMPUTERS IN THE CLASSROOM. Reston, Va.: Reston Publishing Co., 1984.

Bork, Alfred. "Computers in Education Today: and Some Possible Futures." PHI DELTA KAPPAN 66 (December 1984): 239-243.

The author is an outspoken critic of BASIC programming languages. He discusses the presence and influence of computers as they grow within the educational system. He focuses on educational courseware and its low quality while describing how this condition might change. Bork is optimistic and provocative in outling what directions educational courseware might take.

Bunderson, C. Victor, and Gerald W. Faust. "Programmed and Computer-Assisted Instruction." In N.L. Gage, ed. THE PSYCHOLOGY OF TEACHING METHODS. Chicago: University of Chicago, 1976.

Caissy, Gail A. "Evaluating Educational Software: A Practioner's Guide." PHI DELTA KAPPAN 66 (December 1984): 249-250.

Presented is a handy list of guidelines for the educator who has a limited knowledge of computers but who wants to make informed decisions about adopting software for the classroom. The guidelines are grouped into three categories. The first deals with general issues such as what the purpose of the software is and who will be using it. The second contains nine questions that relate to specific elements of instruction such as CAI instructions and reinforcements. The third is a set of four questions that are a continuation of general elements of CAI instruction.

Coburn, P., et al. PRACTICAL GUIDE TO COMPUTERS IN EDUCATION. Reading, Mass.: Addison Wesley Publishing Co., 1982.

Cohen, M.L. "NCSS Looks at the Computer Revolution." SOCIAL EDUCATION 47 (1983): 186-188.

Cohen, Richard, and Robert H. Bradley, "Teaching
Superordinate Concepts with Simulation Games." THE
ALBERTA JOURNAL OF EDUCATIONAL RESEARCH 23 (1977):
298-304

Cohen, Vicki L. Blum. "Criteria for the Evaluation
of Microcomputer Courseware." EDUCATIONAL
TECHNOLOGY 23 (January 1983): 9-13.

Coombs, Don H. "Is There a Future for Simulation
and Gaming Research?" EDUCATIONAL COMMUNICATION AND
TECHNOLOGY JOURNAL 26 (1978): 99-106.

Dayton, Duane K. "Future Trends in the Production
of Instructional Materials: 1981-2001." EDUCATIONAL
COMMUNICATION AND TECHNOLOGY JOURNAL 29 (1981):
231-249.

DeLeeuw, G.J., and N.M. Waters, "Mapping with
Microcomputers in the Elementary Schools." In D.R.
Taylor, ed. EDUCATION AND TRAINING IN CONTEMPORARY
CARTOGRAPHY. New York: John Wiley & Sons, 1985

Begins with a critical look at current elementary
software for teaching mapping skills. An in-depth
look at how LOGO can promote the development of
mapping skills in elementary school-aged children
is the focus of the chapter. It concludes with a
survery of projected developments that are likely
to occur in the area of computer mapping as
practiced in classrooms.

Diem, Richard A. "Computers in the Social Studies
Classroom." HOW TO DO IT SERIES, SERIES 2, NO. 14.
Washington, D.C.: National Council for the Social
Studies, 1981.

Introduces computers to social studies teachers and
suggests ideas for potential applications in the
social studies classroom. A brief but worthwhile
introduction to a variety of related topics.

Elder, C.D. "Problems in the Strucutre and Use of
Educational Simulations." SOCIOLOGY OF EDUCATION 46
(Summer 1973): 335-354.

Ellis, A.B. THE USE AND MISUSE OF COMPUTERS IN
EDUCATION. New York: McGraw-Hill, 1974.

Forman, Denyse. "Search of the Literature." THE
COMPUTING TEACHER 9 (January 1982):43-44.

A brief but provocative synthesis of the literature
regarding the potential, actual, and projected use
of computers in education. Twelve applications are
highlighted. A useful introductory reading on the
topic.

Garner, Dave. "Educational Microcomputer Software:
Nine Questions to Ask." SCIENCE AND CHILDREN 19
(March 1982) 24-25.

Glenn, A.D., and S.J. Rakow. "Computer Simulations:
Effective Teaching Strategies." BYTE (February
1985): 58-59.

Describes the two different types of computer
simulations, stop-time and continuous time, and how
they can be used in the classroom. Gives strategies
for the best time to use a computer simulation for
maximum effectiveness. Suggests classroom
management for a limited number of computers. The
importance of conducting a debriefing session at
the end of a simulation is stressed.

Goodlad, J.I. DYNAMICS OF EDUCATIONAL CHANGE. New
York: McGraw-Hill, 1979.

Greene, M. "Literacy for What?" PHI DELTA KAPPAN 63
(January 1982): 326-329.

Holznagel, Donald C. "Which Courseware for You?"
MICROCOMPUTING 5 (October 1981) 138-140.

Houston, Robert W. "Less Thunder in the Mouth; More
Lightning in the Hand." In Barbara R. Sadwoski and
Charles Lovett, eds. USING COMPUTERS TO ENHANCE
TEACHING AND IMPROVE TEACHING CENTERS. Houston:
University of Houston, 1981.

A general discussion of how computers could affect
education. Seven generalizations are drawn which

cover a variety of issues. Included are comparisons
and contrasts between television and the computer,
the ways that schools may be reorganized, and what
is wrong with the current state of computers and
educational practice.

Ignbar, Michael, and Clarice S. Stoll. SIMULATION
AND GAMING IN SOCIAL SCIENCE. New York: The Free
Press, 1972.

Jay, Timothy B. "The Cognitive Approach to Computer
Courseware Design and Evaluation." EDUCATIONAL
TECHNOLOGY 23 (1983): 22-25.

Komoski, Kenneth P. "Educational Computing: The
Burden of Insuring Quality." PHI DELTA KAPPAN 66
(December 1984): 244-248.

A highly critical review of the state of
educational courseware by the executive director of
EPPI, with major evaluation responsibilites.
Komoski describes some of the reasons behind the
paucity of quality educational software and what
can be done about it. One recommendation is to take
the business of evaluating courseware thoroughly
before purchasing it. Another suggestion concerns
how schools can develop cooperative relationships
with parents to take advantage of the educational
potential of the computer at home.

Lave, Charles A.,and James G. March. AN
INTRODUCTION TO MODELS IN THE SOCIAL SCIENCES. New
York: Harper and Row, 1975.

Lewis, Lawrence T. "All-Purpose Learning Games for
Computer-Assisted Instruction." JOURNAL OF
GEOGRAPHY 78 (November 1979): 237-244.

This is a description of a package of programs
developed to blend entertainment with geography
objectives. Also gives the range of subject matter
and variety of grade levels that the package is
applicable to.

Martorella, Peter H. "Cognition Research: Some
Implications for the Design of Social Studies

Instructional Materials," THEORY AND RESEARCH IN
SOCIAL EDUCATION 10 (1982): 1-16.

Martorella, Peter H., and Dixie Kohn.
"Computer-Related Materials in the Social
Studies/Social Sciences." SOCIAL EDUCATION 34
(December 1970): 899-908.

An article that predates the microcomputer, this
provides an excellent framework for the social
studies educator to use in developing an
understanding of the relationship between the
computer and the social studies. Emphasizes how the
computer can be used as a teaching tool. Also
discussed is how a computer can be used as an
information storage and retrieval device.

Mehaffy, George, Virginia Atwood, and Murry Nelson.
"Action Learning in the Social Studies." In Howard
D. Mehlinger and O.L. Davis, eds. THE SOCIAL
STUDIES. Chicago: National Society for the Study of
Education, 1981.

Merrill, Paul F., and C. Victor Bunderson.
"Preliminary Guidelines for Employing Graphics in
Instruction." JOURNAL OF INSTRUCTIONAL DEVELOPMENT
4 (1981): 2-9.

Nevo, David. "The Conceptualization of Educational
Evaluation: An Analytical Review of the Literature.
REVIEW OF EDUCATIONAL RESEARCH 53 (1983): 117-128.

Newell, Allen. "The Knowledge Level." ARTIFICIAL
INTELLIGENCE 18 (1982): 87-127.

Rawitsch, Don. "Evaluating Computer Courseware:
Even Old Dogs Need Only a Few New Tricks." SOCIAL
EDUCATION 47 (May 1983): 331-332.

A brief discussion of some of the common themes
relevant to computers and education. This includes
sections on locating courseware, evaluation factors
related to instruction, and making sure equipment
matches courseware. This could serve as an
introduction to the basics of courseware
evaluation.

Riordan, Tim. "How to Select Software You Can
Trust." CLASSROOM COMPUTER NEWS 3 (March 1983)
56-61.

Roberts, Nancy, et al. AN INTRODUCTION TO COMPUTER
SIMULATION. Menlo Park, Calif.: Addison-Wesley,
1982.

Roblyer, M.D. "When Is It 'Good Courseware'?
Standards for Microcomputer Courseware."
EDUCATIONAL TECHNOLOGY 21 (October 1981): 27-54.

Schwen, Thomas M. "Professional Scholarship in
Educational Technology: Criteria for Judging
Inquiry." AV COMMUNICATION REVIEW 25 (1977): 5-24.

Sirotnik, Kenneth A. "Evaluating Computer
Courseware." EDUCATIONAL LEADERSHIP 42 (APRIL
1985): 39-42.

A curriculum specialist suggests that software
should be subject to many of the same criteria used
to evaluate any other aspect of the curriculum.
This includes: goals/objectives, content,
strategies, activities, people, materials,
grouping, time, space, and assessment. In addition,
such educational values as equity, experience, and
critical thinking/problem solving should also enter
into the evaluation of CAI. A matrix depicting the
interplay of curriculum criteria and educational
values is presented. The article concludes with
technological issues raised in relation to CAI.

Snyder, Tom, and Jane Palmer. IN SEARCH OF THE MOST
AMAZING THING. Reading, Mass.: Addison-Wesley, in
press.

"The Software Line-Up: What Reviewers Look for When
Evaluating Software." ELECTRONIC LEARNING 2
(October 1982): 45-58.

Stefik, Mark, et al. "The Organization of Expert
Systems: A Tutorial." ARTIFICIAL INTELLIGENCE 18
(1982): 135-173.

Stewart, L.R. "Here's What Classroom Computers Can Do." AMERICAN SCHOOL BOARD JOURNAL 169 (March 1982): 32-45

A useful outline of how computers can be used in nine different subjects, including social studies. Also included are ideas for using the computer to facilitate record keeping in the central office.

Taylor, R., ed. THE COMPUTER IN THE SCHOOL: TUTOR, TOOL, TUTEE. New York: Teachers College Press, 1980.

Tennyson, Robert D. "Interactive Effect of Cognitive Learning Theory with Computer Attributes in the Design of Computer-Assisted Instruction." Paper presented at the Annual Meeting of the American Educational Research Association, Los Angeles (April 1981).

Vargas, Julie S. "Instuctional Design Flaws in Computer-Assisted Instruction." PHI DELTA KAPPAN 67 (June 1986): 738-744

A thorough critique of the differences between well designed and poor instructional practice found in CAI programs. The author describes four basic principles of instructional design that have been drawn from the large body of literature that exists on the topic. Various forms of CAI, such as drill and practice, tutorials, and simulations, are examined in light of the four basic principles outlined. Examples from programs commonly found illustrate what the author considers flaws in instructional design.

Wager, Walter. "Design Considerations for Instructional Computing Programs." JOURNAL OF EDUCATIONAL TECHNOLOGY SYSTEMS 10 (1982): 261-269.

Weible, T.D., and Jacqueline McHahon. "Using Microcomputers in the Social Studies." THE SOCIAL STUDIES 73 (May/June 1982): 110-113.

A detailed description of how the authors created a microcomputer simulation for secondary social studies students. The topic is the Depression and decision making is emphasized. An element of chance is introduced into many of the players' options which makes this a very realistic simulation. An excellent description of how a social studies simulation operates and serves to motivate students.

White, Mary Alice. "Synthesis of Research on Electronic Learning." EDUCATIONAL LEADERSHIP 40 (May 1983): 11-15.

CHAPTER 4

AN ANNOTATED BIBLIOGRAPHY

OF SOCIAL STUDIES SOFTWARE

This chapter is intended to provide the reader with a selected survey of the available social studies software. The particular programs that are included were chosen on the basis of popularity, educational effectiveness, flexibility for grouping, or because they were representative of the various subject areas within the social studies. Programs for elementary and secondary social studies are included. Obviously, it is nearly an impossible task to keep up with all the social studies software that is being created and distributed. It is hoped that the software reviewed in this chapter will help the social studies teacher in the search for the most educationally effective software.

Each review has the most up-to-date information available. This includes the grade level(s) that the publisher has listed as the intended target for the program. The reader should be cautioned that this is often only an estimate by the software producer and in some cases programs could be used with students either above or below the suggested grade level. This, of course, is dependent on the abilities and interests of the students using the program.

A suggested group size is given for each program, and this ranges one from individual through the entire class. Many programs were intended by the publishers to be used individually by students. Often, however, this presents a logistical nightmare for the teacher who has a class of thirty students who could all benefit from working with a particular program. Where appropriate I have indicated when students could work in small groups. In this case between two and five students to a group is recommended to complete

a program. Ultimately, a teacher's classroom
management ability should be the final determiner
of how many students in a group should be allowed
to work on a given program. The social studies
teacher should not lose sight of the fact that when
students work as a group valuable social skills,
such as working towards consensus or taking turns
can be promoted. Students will often need some
guidance and structure to function effectively as a
unit.

The current cost of software is not included
in the review because this is subject to frequent
change due to market conditions. The current price
can best be obtained by writing or calling the
software publisher directly. When available,
references for additional reviews of programs are
given at the end of each entry. These references,
and the reviews contained in this chapter, should
not be substituted for an in-depth evaluation by
the reader before purchasing any program. While
every effort has been made to be as thorough,
objective, and accurate as possible, the classroom
teacher must ultimately decide whether a given
piece of software will be compatible with the
objectives of the social studies curriculum and,
more importantly, meet the needs of the students
who are using it.

PROGRAM TITLE: AFRICA

GRADE LEVEL: 7-14   GROUP: individual or small

PUBLISHER: Educational Activities
           P.O. Box 392
           Freeport, NY 11520
           (800) 645-3739

SYSTEM REQUIREMENTS: Apple II+, IIe/48K/disk
drive/Applesoft BASIC/ DOS 3.3

Commodore PET/16K/ disk drive/BASIC

TRS 80 Model III or IV/32K/ disk drive/TRS-DOS

PACKAGE INCLUDES: 2 program diskettes (with
backup), documentation (10 pp.)

INSTRUCTIONAL MODE: tutorial, drill and practice

SUBJECT: geography

COMMENTS: A two-disk program, the first is a tutorial that teaches general information and geographical facts about Africa. Special attention is paid to dispel common misconceptions children often hold about this continent. The second disk contains a series of map drill quizzes on countries, major cities, and physical features. The documentation is adequate and the overall program consistently receives high ratings from reviewers.

PROGRAM TITLE: AGENT USA

GRADE LEVEL: 4 and up   GROUP: individual or small

PUBLISHER: Scholastic, Inc.
           730 Broadway
           New York, NY 10003
           (212) 505-3502

SYSTEM REQUIREMENTS: Apple II+ or IIe/48K/disk drive/Applesoft BASIC

Atari 400, 800, or 1200/48K/disk drive/BASIC

Commodore 64/disk drive/BASIC

IBM PC or jr/64K/disk drive/BASIC

PACKAGE INCLUDES: 1 program diskette (with backup), instruction manual (23 pp.), teacher's guide (16 pp.), map board, posters, stickers

INSTRUCTIONAL MODE: simulation and educational game

SUBJECT: geography

COMMENTS: Students are required to read and interpret time schedules, maps, and train routes as they pretend to be super sleuths for the CIA who travel around the country. The mission is to find and disarm the FussBomb before it does its damage.

The program begins with a brief demonstration which
is minimally helpful. Also of little help to the
students is the documentation which requires a
teacher's guidance. The game takes a long time to
complete, but it is an exciting, entertaining way
to teach children valuable map reading skills such
as interpreting map symbols, finding location and
direction.

ADDITIONAL REVIEWS: Lazerick, Beth. TEACHING AND
COMPUTERS (October 1984): 64.

O'Malley, Christopher. PERSONAL SOFTWARE (June
1984): 6.

PROGRAM TITLE: AMERICAN HISTORY ADVENTURE

GRADE LEVEL: 7-12   GROUP: individual or small

PUBLISHER: Intellectual Software
           798 North Ave.
           Bridgeport, CT 06606
           (800) 232-2224

SYSTEM REQUIREMENTS: Apple II, II+, or IIe/48K/disk
drive

IBM PC or jr/48K/disk drive

PACKAGE INCLUDES: 1 diskette (backups available at
extra cost), teacher's guide (5 pp.)

INSTRUCTIONAL MODE: drill and practice

SUBJECT: history

COMMMENTS: Students assume the role of a reporter
traveling through time to interview famous people
in our nation's past. To be successful, the player
must review historical data as they try to identify
the ninety-two figures that are presented in the
program. An extremely easy-to-read program, it will
require little assistance from the teacher. The
teacher's guide that accompanies it is of value.
The program is designed to emphasize memorization
rather than critical thinking.

PROGRAM TITLE: AMERICAN HISTORY: THE DECADES GAME

GRADE LEVEL: 9 and up   GROUP: individual or small

PUBLISHER: Brain Bank, Inc.
           220 Fifth Ave.
           New York, NY 10001
           (212) 686-6565

SYSTEM REQUIREMENTS: Apple II+, IIe, or
IIc/48K/disk drive

Commodore PET/16K

PACKAGE INCLUDES: 1 program diskette (backup
available at extra cost), teacher's guide (8 pp.),
supplementary materials

INSTRUCTIONAL MODE: drill and practice

SUBJECT: American history

COMMENTS: Dates of events in American politics,
economics, technology, science, and arts are
highlighted as players learn historical data. A
competitive approach is used to help motivate
students and reduce drudgery. The accompanying
content is good. The over reliance on memorizing
dates, however, does not develop critical thinking
or other higher order cognitive skills.

PROGRAM TITLE: ARCHEOLOGY SEARCH

GRADE LEVEL: 5-9   GROUP: class

PUBLISHER: McGraw Hill Book Company
           1221 Avenue of the Americas
           New York, NY 10020
           (800) 223-4180

SYSTEM REQUIREMENTS: Apple II, II+, IIe/48K/disk
drive/Applesoft BASIC

TRS-80 MODEL III OR IV/disk drive/BASIC

PACKAGE INCLUDES: 1 diskette with backup, teacher's

guide (24 pp.), 20 student workbooks (32 pp.)

INSTRUCTIONAL MODE: simulation, logic, and problem solving

SUBJECT: archeology

COMMENTS: Using data from objects discovered at a historic colonial site, student teams devise theories about the people who once lived there. This includes having students perform tests, evaluate results, and draw conclusions. The use of graphics is above average in this program. Also of note are clear instructions. Problem-solving skills such as evidence gathering, record keeping, evaluation of evidence, risk taking, and synthesis are taught. Student mistakes are also well handled by the program which further facilitates problem solving. The accompanying workbooks are superior and the program lends itself to full class involvement.

ADDITIONAL REVIEWS: Biro, Charles. BOOKLIST 80 (March 1, 1984): 1002.

Boston, B.O. INFOWORLD REPORT CARD (December 1, 1983): 96-97.

Owens, Peter. POPULAR COMPUTING 2 (October 1983): 220-228.

PROGRAM TITLE: BEYOND THE RISING SUN - DISCOVERING JAPAN

GRADE LEVEL: 7-adult   GROUP: individual or small

PUBLISHER: Educational Activities, Inc.
          Freeport, NY 11520
          (800) 645-3739

SYSTEM REQUIREMENTS: Apple II+, IIe, IIc/disk drive/48K

PACKAGE INCLUDES: 1 diskette (with backup), teacher's guide (14 pp.)

INSTRUCTIONAL MODE: simulation, drill and practice

SUBJECT: geography, multicultural education

COMMENTS: The object of the simulation is to become
a successful member of Japanese society. The
players may choose either a male or female role and
play begins with the high school and progresses
through college, marriage, and early adulthood. To
be successful the players must accumulate points as
they make decisions in three categories: money,
success, and family harmony. The simulation does
help the learner become familiar with certain
values of Japanese society. For maximum educational
effectiveness the teacher has to supplement the
simulation with additional information and learning
activities.

PROGRAM TITLE: CARTEL AND CUTTHROATS

GRADE LEVEL: 8 and up   GROUP: individual or small

PUBLISHER: Strategic Simulations, Inc.
            456 Fairchild Drive, Suite 108
            Mountain View, CA 94043
            (415) 964-1353

SYSTEM REQUIREMENTS: Apple II+/48K/disk
drive/Applesoft BASIC/game paddles/printer

PACKAGE INCLUDES: 1 program diskette, teacher's
guide (14 pp.), business planning pad, short rule
cards

INSTRUCTIONAL MODE: educational game, simulation

SUBJECT: economics, business

COMMENTS: A sophisticated management simulation
which assumes student familiarity with such
concepts and terms as GNP, CPI, prime rate, etc.
Students run a simulated manufacturing company that
buys raw materials, produces finished goods, and
sells the goods in a competitive market. Overall,
an excellent program. One shortcoming is the
program's poor error trapping or inability to

prevent the player from inputting incorrect information. It is also a time consuming program requring some ten hours of total playing time. Players, however, can save current game for later use. Maximum educational effectiveness requires teacher preparation.

ADDITIONAL REVIEWS: Humphries, Terry. COURSEWARE REPORT CARD (September 1982).

MICROSIFT (May 1983).

White, Charles. ELECTRONIC LEARNING 4 (September 1984): 61.

Unwin, Graham, and Mollie Cohen. ELECTRONIC LEARNING 2 (November/December 1982): 81-82.

PROGRAM TITLE: CHOICE OR CHANCE

GRADE LEVEL: 7-9   GROUP: individual or small

PUBLISHER: Rand McNally & Co.
           8255 N. Central Park Avenue
           Skokie, IL 60676
           (312) 673-9100

SYSTEM REQUIREMENTS: Apple II+, IIe, IIc/48K/disk drive

PACKAGE INCLUDES: 2 program diskettes (backups available at extra cost), teacher's guide (10 pp.), student workbook (38 pp.)

INSTRUCTIONAL MODE: simulation

SUBJECT: history and geography

COMMENTS: Three history simulations are included in this excellent supplementary program to junior high level American history. Success in the simulations is based on the players' ability to make decisions about a course of action. The importance and role of geography is emphasized in the simulations, which are: Exploration and Colonization, The Expansion Period, and The Industrialization Period.

The reproducible worksheets that accompany each
simulation are excellent supplementary materials.
An easy program to use, the content and
instructional technique make this package
educationally useful.

PROGRAM TITLE: COMMUNITY SEARCH

GRADE LEVEL: 4 and up   GROUP: class

PUBLISHER: McGraw-Hill Book Company
           1221 Avenue of the Americas
           New York, NY 10020
           (800) 223-4180

SYSTEM REQUIREMENTS: Apple II+, IIe, or
IIc/48K/disk drive/ Applesoft BASIC

TRS-80 Model III or IV/48K/disk drive/BASIC

PACKAGE INCLUDES: 1 diskette (with backup),
teacher's guide, 20 student workbooks

INSTRUCTIONAL MODE: simulation

SUBJECT: economics

COMMENTS: Students are placed in the role of a
council of elders of a primitive society forced to
leave its homeland. Their task is to make choices
about where to migrate, what occupations to pursue,
and how to use resources wisely. The class is
divided into teams. It is at this level that much
social studies learning occurs as the students
research and participate in discussions while
working their way through the simulation. The
teacher's materials are very well developed and are
accompanied by numerous supplementary activites. An
excellent interactive program that could easily be
used with fifth through eighth grades. The program
seems interesting enough to motivate lower
achieving high school students.

ADDITIONAL REVIEWS: Boston, B.O. INFOWORLD REPORT
CARD (December 1, 1983): 81-82.

Owens, Peter. POPULAR COMPUTING 2 (October 1983): 220-228.

Unwin, Graham. CREATIVE COMPUTING 9 (October 1983): 152.

Unwin, Graham, and Mollie Cohen. ELECTRONIC LEARNING 2 (November/December 1982): 81-82.

PROGRAM TITLE: CROSSCOUNTRY USA

GRADE LEVEL: 5-8 GROUP: individual or small

PUBLISHER: Didatech Software Limited
          549 - 810 West Broadway
          Vancouver, BC Canada
          V5Z 4C9
          (604) 687-3468

SYSTEM REQUIREMENTS: Apple II, II+, or IIe/64K/disk drive/color monitor recommended/ printer optional

PACKAGE INCLUDES: 1 program diskette, 1 graphics diskette (user makes backup), 10 student maps, 1 classroom map, documentation (30 pp.)

INSTRUCTIONAL MODE: simulation

SUBJECT: economics, geography

COMMENTS: This interactive program has the user simulate a truck driver's route. Over 52 different commodities can be picked up and delivered to one of 180 U.S. cities where the commodities are vital to the local economy. Commodities are revealed through the use of thought provoking clues which help the user learn of the uses of the commodities involved. The driver must also buy gas, eat, and sleep along the way. The program keeps track of time and expenses. Similarly, traffic violations and accidents are figured into the driver's account. The program is appealing to students because it is challenging and has some clever graphics. The documentation is well written.

PROGRAM TITLE: DECISIONS DECISIONS

GRADE LEVEL: 6-12   GROUP: small or large groups

PUBLISHER: Tom Snyder Productions, Inc.
          123 Mt. Auburn St.
          Cambridge, MA 02138
          (617) 876-4433

SYSTEM REQUIREMENTS: Will be available for Apple
and IBM. Contact the publisher for specific
details.

PACKAGE INCLUDES: Documentation will vary depending
on which package is being used. Each package will
consist of a student guide, teacher guide,
reference guide and diskette with backup.

INSTRUCTIONAL MODE: simulation

SUBJECT: contemporary issues

COMMENTS: Designed for use in an average size class
where only one computer is available. The only
program from this series currrently available is
called "Aftermath" which places students in small
groups where they simulate a public relations team
for a company that is advertising on a
controversial corporate TV program dealing with
nuclear war. The students must set priorities for a
course of action. As the simulation advances, the
situation becomes more complicated requiring
further values exploration and small group
discussion about the controversy. Students are
referred to a player's guide which contains
historically relevant data that they also consider.
About the only drawback is the small size of the
graphic displays. Overall, an excellent simulation
but will require additional classroom management on
the teacher's part. Similarly, the teacher should
set the stage and conclude the activity with
class-wide discussion. Future simulations are being
created around themes such as national security in
a democracy, life in colonial America, and the
Industrial Revolution.

PROGRAM TITLE: THE DECISION SHOP

GRADE LEVEL: 4-8   GROUP: individual, small, or
large group

PUBLISHER: The Children's Museum of Indianapolis
           c/o Dr. Marianne Talafuse
           Center for Economic Education
           146 WB, Ball State University
           Muncie, IN 47306

SYSTEM REQUIREMENTS: Apple II, II+, or IIe/disk
drive/ Applesoft BASIC/DOS 3.3

PACKAGE INCLUDES: 1 diskette (with backup)

INSTRUCTIONAL MODE: drill and practice, simulation,
tutorial

SUBJECT: economics

COMMENTS: There are three programs contained on the
diskette. "Kingdom" involves the purchase and sale
of land, planting of wheat crops, and feeding of
the population. "Star Trader" involves balancing
the distribution of food, air, fuel, and water for
a space colony. "Sell Robots" is designed to help
the learner calculate the optimum selling price
through trial and error followed by a tutorial
review. The package is fun and challenging.
Students can see the results as they manipulate
variables and observe the interaction that takes
place. The presentation of the content is clear and
logical. The programs assume whole number
operations and an upper elementary school reading
ability. It is a short program, taking between
twenty to thirty minutes to complete.
Unfortunately, there are no support materials.

PROGRAM TITLE: DEMO-GRAPHICS

GRADE LEVEL: 8-up   GROUP: individual, small, or
class

PUBLISHER: Conduit
           P.O. Box 388

Iowa City, Iowa 52244
(319) 353-5789

SYSTEM REQUIREMENTS: Apple II, II+, IIe/48K/disk
drive/DOS 3.1 or 3.3

PACKAGE INCLUDES: 1 diskette (with backup),
instruction manual, sample program output, and
teacher's guide

INSTRUCTIONAL MODE: tutorial, simulation

SUBJECT: population studies, demographics

COMMENTS: The disk contains five programs:
"Introduction Program," "Age Pyramids," "Population
vs. Time Plots," "General Program," and "Country
Editing Program." It would take the average student
about thirty minutes a day for a week to work
through the five programs. The purpose of the
programs is to demonstrate the differential impact
of fertility rates and mortality on aging. Students
can compare age standardized birth and death rates
for the populations of a number of countries. The
construction of various fertiltiy and mortality
rate charts can be undertaken. This immediate
viewing of the results of changing population
related variables is a strong point. The package is
motivational and the use of the computer's graphics
capabilites is excellent.

PROGRAM TITLE: ENERGY SEARCH

GRADE LEVEL: 5-9   GROUP: class

PUBLISHER: McGraw-Hill Book Company
           1221 Avenue of the Americas
           New York, NY 10020
           (800) 223-4180

SYSTEM REQUIREMENTS: APPLE II, II+, or IIe/48K/disk
drive/Applesoft BASIC

TRS-80 Model III or IV/48K/disk drive/BASIC

PACKAGE INCLUDES: 1 program diskette (with backup),

teacher's guide (32 pp.), 20 student workbooks

INSTRUCTIONAL MODE: simulation

SUBJECT: energy, resources, and development

COMMENTS: Students learn about problem solving as
they apply basic reading, math, science, and social
studies skills. This occurs as the players engage
in a simulation that involves them in the
management of an energy factory. The program is set
up to accommodate one hundred different user groups
and may take between six and a dozen class periods
to complete. The supporting materials are a
strength of this package. The reading in the
sourcebook and the graphs, charts, and diagrams are
excellent learning experiences as they are an
outstanding introduction to these kinds of tools.
Students employ a variety of learning strategies,
including using encyclopedias, observing others,
and trial and error while working through this
superior learning package.

ADDITIONAL REVIEWS: Boston, Bruce. INFOWORLD REPORT
CARD (December 1, 1983): 96-97.

CLASSROOM COMPUTING NEWS 2 (January/February 1982):
42.

Owens, Peter. POPULAR COMPUTING 2 (October 1983):
220-228.

PROGRAM TITLE: GEOGRAPHY SEARCH

GRADE LEVEL: 4 and up   GROUP: small or entire class

PUBLISHER: McGraw-Hill Book Company
           1221 Avenue of the Americas
           New York, NY 10020
           (800) 223-4180

SYSTEM REQUIREMENTS: Apple II, II+, IIe, or
IIc/48K/disk drive/Applesoft BASIC

TRS-80 MODEL III/32K/disk drive/BASIC

PACKAGE INCLUDES: 1 diskette (with backup), teacher's manual (21 pp.), 20 student workbooks (30 pp.)

INSTRUCTIONAL MODE: simulation

SUBJECT: geography

COMMENTS: Groups of students are put on ancient ships searching for the New World. An extensive unit of study, this program will require considerable teacher preparation and between six and twelve weeks of student use to gain maximum benefit. This will provide for an in-depth understanding of direction and location concepts and skills. Information processing skills are fostered on several levels. At the end of each session of play, the computer provides information that the team must use to chart their position and decide on the next course of action. The clear and well-structured student booklets that accompany the program provide the background material that students master in the process of working through the package.

ADDITIONAL REVIEWS: Bockman, Fred. ELECTRONIC LEARNING 1 (January/February 1982): 72.

Cohen, Mollie. THE COMPUTING TEACHER 10 (December 1982): 49-51.

Grinder, Michael. CHIME NEWSLETTER (July/August 1984).

Hively, Wells. ELECTRONIC EDUCATION 3 (January 1984): 22-23.

Owens, Peter. POPULAR COMPUTING 2 (October 1983): 220-228.

White, Charles. SOCIAL EDUCATION 47 (May 1983): 338-342.

Woldman, Evelyn. TEACHING AND COMPUTERS (January 1985): 56-57.

Wood, Irene. BOOKLIST 79 (April 1, 1983): 1047.

PROGRAM TITLE: INTRODUCTION TO ECONOMICS

GRADE LEVEL: 8-adult   GROUP: individual, small, or class

PUBLISHER: MECC
           3490 Lexington Avenue, North
           St. Paul, MN 55112
           (612) 481-3500

SYSTEM REQUIREMENTS: Apple II+, IIe, or IIc/dual disk drives/Pioneer VP-1000, Sylvania 7200, or Magnavox 8010 optical videodisc player

PACKAGE INCLUDES: 1 videodisc, teacher's manual, students' manual, interface card, teacher diskette, nine curriculum diskettes

INSTRUCTIONAL MODE: tutorial, simulation

SUBJECT: economics

COMMENTS: Designed to deliver an entire high school course, this is a state of the art use of "interactive video." There is a total of 25 sessions lasting anywhere from 30-50 minutes. Guided by the computer, the student works through computer tutorials and questions, workbook exercises, and videodisc viewing assignments. It is reasonably simple for a teacher to administer the data files, a desirable quality. The program is, however, expensive and requires equipment not typically found in high schools.

ADDITIONAL REVIEWS: Kessinger, Phil. THE COMPUTING TEACHER 12 (December/January 1984-85): 36-39.

PROGRAM TITLE: JENNY OF THE PRAIRIE

GRADE LEVEL: 1-6   GROUP: individual or small

PUBLISHER: Rhinannon/Computer Games for Girls
           3717 Titan Drive
           Richmond, VA 23225
           (804) 272-7770

SYSTEM REQUIREMENTS: Apple II, II+, or IIe/48K/disk drive/Compiled BASIC

PACKAGE INCLUDES: 1 diskette, teacher's guide (2 pp.)

INSTRUCTIONAL MODE: game, logic, and problem solving

SUBJECT: pioneer women, wilderness survival

COMMENTS: This story involves the player(s) in an attempt to help a pioneer girl survive her first winter alone after being separated from her family. Shelter, food, warmth, and safety are among the problems she must solve before the onslaught of winter. There are nine screens, each with three levels of difficulty. Students are intrigued by the colorful graphics and the opportunity to explore an imaginary landscape with their "computer-aged" doll. The games are nonviolent and often involve role-playing. Younger students would probably need help reading the text.

ADDITIONAL REVIEW: Bumgarner, M. A. CLASSROOM COMPUTER LEARNING 4 (February 1984): 63-65.

Imhoff, Heidi. THE COMPUTING TEACHER 11 (April 1, 1984): 35.

Mace, Scott. INFOWORLD 4 (April 30, 1982): 41.

Milich, Melissa. SOFTALK (August 1983): 168-170.

PROGRAM TITLE: THE LANGUAGE OF MAPS (SERIES A & B)

GRADE LEVEL: 4-8   GROUP: individual, small, or class

PUBLISHER: Focus Media, Inc.
          839 Stewart Avenue
          Garden City, NY 11530
          (800) 645-8989

SYSTEM REQUIREMENTS: Apple II, II+, IIe, IIc/48K/disk drive/color monitor

PACKAGE INCLUDES: 3 diskettes, instructor's manual
for each series (23 pp.), and support materials (9
pp.)

INSTRUCTIONAL MODE: tutorial

SUBJECT: geography

COMMENTS: A good use of graphics and the computer's
tutorial potential. Series A consists of three
disks covering the following: oceans and
continents; land areas and water bodies; and
highlands and lowlands. Series B also has three
disks which include: finding your way on maps;
finding places on maps; and measuring distances.
The instructional approach is sound, e.g.,
misspellings are indicated as such but not counted
as incorrect answers. The graphics reinforce the
concept being taught.

PROGRAM TITLE: LINCOLN'S DECISIONS

GRADE LEVEL: 7 and up   GROUP: individual or small

PUBLISHER: Educational Activities, Inc.
           P.O. Box 392
           Freeport, NY 11520
           (516) 223-4666

SYSTEM REQUIREMENTS: Apple II, II+, or IIe/48k/disk
drive/Applesoft BASIC

Commodore 64/disk drive/BASIC

TRS-80 Model III/32k/ disk drive/BASIC

PACKAGE INCLUDES: 1 diskette (with a backup),
teacher's guide (16 pp.)

INSTRUCTIONAL MODE: simulation, drill and practice

SUBJECT: United States history (1861-65), Civil War

COMMENTS: This program acquaints students with the
events of Lincoln's life and administration.
Explanatory text is accompanied by useful maps and

time lines. The documentation includes a list of
follow-up activites and questions. It is not useful
as a decision making program, however; there is
little to encourage inductive reasoning. Still,
this is a very useful program for studying that
time period. It is more drill and practice then a
true simulation. As drill and practice, however, it
is educationally valid.

ADDITONAL REVIEWS: Bitter, Gary. INSTRUCTOR 93
(November/December 1983): 94-96.

CLASSROOM COMPUTER LEARNING 4 (January 1984):
52-56.

Crites, Jana S. THE BOOK WORLD 17
(November/December 1983): 62.

Dana, Ana. TEACHING AND COMPUTERS (October 1983):
64.

Hively, Wells. ELECTRONIC EDUCATION 3
(November/December 1984): 41.

Jackson, R.W. MICROCOMPUTERS IN EDUCATION (Otober
1983): 14.

Marran. J.F. CURRICULUM REVIEW 23 (April 1984):
103-104.

McCarley, Barbara. EDUCATIONAL TECHNOLOGY 23
(November 1983): 56-58.

Wood, Irene. BOOKLIST 80 (November 1983): 438-439.

PROGRAM TITLE: MAP READING

GRADE LEVEL: 4-7   GROUP: individual or small group

PUBLISHER: Micro Power and Light Company
           12820 Hillcrest Rd.
           Suite 244
           Dallas, TX 75220
           (214) 239-6620

SYSTEM REQUIREMENTS: Apple II+/disk

drive/Applesoft/DOS 3.2

PACKAGE INCLUDES: 1 diskette, teacher's guide, and supplementary material

INSTRUCTIONAL MODE: tutorial, drill and practice

SUBJECT: geography

COMMENTS: Students will need to be able to multiply single digit whole numbers in order to work with this program. It takes approximately 100 minutes to complete the program. The program is most useful for introducing or reinforcing map reading skills, particularly using the compass. The program is relatively inexpensive and has merit. The lack of record keeping and minor inconsistencies in user-directions are slight drawbacks. Students would profit from additional work on the objectives as the level of difficulty is not particularly challenging.

PROGRAM TITLE: THE MARKET PLACE

GRADE LEVEL: 3-8   GROUP: individual, small, or entire class

PUBLISHER: MECC
           3490 Lexington Avenue
           St. Paul, MN 55112
           (612) 481-3500

SYSTEM REQUIREMENTS: APPLE II+, IIe, or IIc/48K/disk drive/Applesoft BASIC

Atari 400, 800, 600XL, 800XL, or 1200XL/48K/disk drive/BASIC

TRS-80 Color computer/48K/disk drive/Extended BASIC

PACKAGE INCLUDES: 1 diskette - four programs (with backup), instruction manual (49-75 pp.)

INSTRUCTIONAL MODE: simulation

SUBJECT: economics

COMMENTS: A popular program with MECC users, it is designed to teach elementary economic concepts such as the relationship between production, advertising, and prices in small businesses. After some prior discussion about the concepts of supply and demand, production, price, and estimation, advanced students could work individually with the program as an enrichment. Feedback from the program develops and clarifies understanding.

PROGRAM TITLE: THE MEDALISTS - STATES

GRADE LEVEL: 4-10   GROUP: individual or small

PUBLISHER: Hartley Courseware, Inc.
P.O. Box 419
Dimondale, MI 48821

SYSTEM REQUIREMENTS: Apple II+, IIe, IIc/48K/disk drive/Applesoft/DOS 3.3

PACKAGE INCLUDES: 1 diskette, user's guide (26 pp.)

INSTRUCTIONAL MODE: drill and practice, game

SUBJECT: geography

COMMENTS: To be successful students must have learned some basic facts about the states. Students can set the level of difficulty. Questions cover such topics as postal abbreviations, bordering states, major industries, state birds, and state capital. Equipped to keep records for up to 50 students, the programs can probably be reused repeatedly by students in 15 to 50-minute sessions. Most appropriate for students in the middle level of schooling, the program has the capacity to add content items. Misspellings are not pointed out to students.

PROGRAM TITLE: MEET THE PRESIDENTS

GRADE LEVEL 4-12   GROUP: individual, small, or class

PUBLISHER: Versa Computing
3541 Old Conejo Road
Suite 104
Newbury Park, CA 91320
(805) 498-1956

SYSTEM REQUREMENTS: Apple II, II+, IIe, or
IIc/48K/disk drive/Applesoft BASIC and Machine
language

PACKAGE INCLUDES: 4 diskettes, instruction manual
(4 pp.)

INSTRUCTIONAL MODE: drill and practice, game

SUBJECT: U.S. history, politics, and government

COMMENTS: Using high resolution graphics, this
program slowly creates an image of a president
while giving clues to his identity. Score is based
on the amount of time it takes a student to guess
correct person. A very friendly program that
provides only positive reinforcement by ignoring
incorrect responses. Also accepts divergent
spellings. Teachers can modify this program, making
it very attractive.

ADDTIONAL REVIEW: Dana, Ann. TEACHING AND COMPUTERS
(January 1984): 60.

Heller, Cyndi. CUE NEWSLETTER (May 1984): 23.

PROGRAM TITLE: MILLIONAIRE

GRADE LEVEL: 9 and up   GROUP: individual, small,
or class

PUBLISHER: Blue Chip Software
6744 Eton Avenue
Canoga Park, CA 91303
(818) 346-0730

SYSTEM REQUIRMENTS: Apple IIe, IIc, or III/64K/disk
drive/Interpreter BASIC

Commodore 64/disk dirve/Interpreter BASIC

IBM PC or jr/MS-DOS/128K/disk drive/Compiled BASIC

Macintosh/128K/disk drive PASCAL

PACKAGE INCLUDES: 1 diskette, instruction manual
(22 pp.)

INSTRUCTIONAL MODE: simulation

SUBJECT: economics

COMMENTS: As a novice on the New York Stock
Exchange the player is given $10,000 and a range of
15 actual stocks. The object is to successfully buy
and sell in response to an array of influences on
the market. As a student becomes more successful,
new and riskier options, such as buying stocks on
margin and put and call, are added. The simulation
does a more than adequate job with short-term
investments, but, unfortunately, it ignores
long-term aspects of the stock market. The
accompanying materials provide stock market tips
but ignore some fundamentals like capitalization of
price-earning ratios. Overall, a worthwhile
program.

ADDITIONAL REVIEWS: Eicholz, R.L. CLASSROOM
COMPUTER LEARNING (September 1984): 19.

Johnson, Forrest. SOFTALK (December 1983): 358.

Sherouse, Vicki. BOOKLIST 80 (May 1, 1984): 1264.

Strehlo, Kevin. PERSONAL SOFTWARE (February 1984):
60-61, 63.

PROGRAM TITLE: THE OTHER SIDE

GRADE LEVEL: 7 and up   GROUP: small

PUBLISHER: Tom Snyder Productions
           123 Mount Auburn Street
           Cambridge, MA 02138
           (617) 876-4433

SYSTEM REQUIREMENTS:Apple II +, IIe, and

IIc/48k/disk drive

IBM PC, PCjr

Commodore 64

modems optional, color monitor recommended

PACKAGE INCLUDES:
1 diskette (with backup), 2 resource guides (23
pp.), 2 players' guides (24 pp.), game board and
pen

INSTRUCTIONAL MODE: simulation

SUBJECT: political science, global studies

COMMENTS: The microworld created in this simulation
involves the player in the search for three types
of fuel as a member of one of two nations that rule
the world. The object is to complete a bridge
between these two countries and this can be
achieved in either a competitive or cooperative
mode. Each mode drastically alters the course of
the simulation. Each side is given income which
should be invested in drilling for the fuels. In
either country as the fuels are mixed bridge
building can occur. An intriguing variable
possessed by each side is C.A.D., a Computer
Assisted Defense system. C.A.D. monitors the
economy of the respective side as well as
international developments. If a threat is
perceived, C.A.D. can step in and take over play
and the results may not be to the liking of the
player(s) on the affected side. This simulation can
be used with a modem which means games could be
played between teams at different sites.
The program is not easily learned, but well worth
the time involved.

ADDITIONAL REVIEWS: Field, C. E. INCIDER 4 (January
1986): 64-66.

Fougerat, Billie. "Summitry for Students."
ELECTRONIC LEARNING 5 (November/December 1985): 54.

Olds, F. H. CLASSROOM COMPUTING LEARNING 5
(April/May): 21.

Rathje, Linda. THE COMPUTING TEACHER 13 (October 1985): 49-51.

Rotenberg, Lesli. "Classroom Happenings." TEACHING AND COMPUTERS 3 (February 1986): 33.

PROGRAM TITLE: POLITICAL GENIE

GRADE LEVEL: 6 and up   GROUP: individual or small

PUBLISHER: Boring Software Company
P.O. Box 568
Boring, OR 97009
(503) 663-4464

SYSTEM REQUIREMENTS: Apple IIe, IIc/128K/80 column card/disk drive/monitor

IBM PC or jr/128K/disk drive/DOS 2.1

PACKAGE INCLUDES: 1 program diskette, 6 data diskettes, documentation (70 pp.), response sheet (unlimited reproduction)

INSTRUCTIONAL MODE: simulation, tutorial

SUBJECT: political science, history, geography

COMMENTS: This program shows how congressional members from the 50 states voted on a variety of 100 issues including civil rights, foreign policy, taxation, education, and defense. The program is closed and additional information cannot be added by the teacher. Students can choose the issues that are important to them and up to eight students can participate at once by recording their votes on a separate response form. Pre-voting discussion is encouraged and "pro" and "con" positions are provided from selected congressional members. Biographical information about congressional representatives is available for the database. How an individual member and how the entire House or Senate voted on an issue are provided in graph form. A graph is displayed after students have voted on each issue. The documentation is thorough and divided into a teaching guide and technical section.

PROGRAM TITLE: PRESIDENT ELECT

GRADE LEVEL: 6 and up   GROUP: individual or small

PUBLISHER: Strategic Simulations, Inc.
883 Stierlin Road, Building A-200
Mountain View, CA 94043
(415) 964-1353

SYSTEM REQUIREMENTS: Apple II, II+, IIe, IIc, or
II/48K/disk drive/ Applesoft BASIC

Commodore 64/disk drive/BASIC

PACKAGE INCLUDES: 1 diskette, instruction manual (9
pp.), planning pads, short rules sheet

INSTRUCTIONAL MODE: simulation

SUBJECT: U.S. history, presidents

COMMENTS: A very well designed simulation described
by some as "a must during an election year."
Players are responsible for managing a candidate's
campaign and are successful depending on their
abilities to select strategies. It is necessary to
consider inherent strengths and weakenesses of
one's candidate, chance events, and the
pre-campaign situation. The program is permeated
with a wry humor. To take full advantage of all the
materials and learning possiblities, teachers
should plan to spend 2 1/2 to 3 weeks on the
simulation.
ADDITIONAL REVIEWS: Goles, G.G. EDUCATIONAL
COMPUTER MAGAZINE (January/February 1983): 44.

Hively, Wells. ELECTRONIC EDUCATION 3
(November/December 1984): 40-41.

Lechner, Jack. GAMES (December 1984): 51.

White, Charles S. SOCIAL EDUCATION 47 (May 1983):
338-339.

PROGRAM TITLE: RAILS WEST

GRADE LEVEL: 9 - 12   GROUP: individual, small, or class

PUBLISHER: Strategic Simulations, Inc.
            833 Stierlin Road, Building A200
            Mountain View, CA 94043
            (415) 964-1353

SYSTEM REQUIREMENTS: Apple II, II+, or IIe/48K/disk drive/Applesoft BASIC

Atari 800/48K/disk drive/Basic

Commodore 64/disk drive/BASIC

PACKAGE INCLUDES: 1 diskette, instruction manual (16 pp.), a "Starting Railroads" reference board, and a pad of score sheets

INSTRUCTIONAL MODE: simulation

SUBJECT: history, economics

COMMENTS: An engrossing simulation that has the players attempting to build a railroad empire through decision making, application of economic principles, and even sabotage of the competition. There is an option for the number of players and games can be saved so there is no time limitation. The documentation is not as clear about aspects of game playing as it could be. The teacher needs to engage the students in prior learning about economic phenomena such as stocks, bonds, securities, and loans. If elementary and middle school students can master the terminology it could be used in a gifted and talented program.

ADDITIONAL REVIEWS: Lechner, Jack. GAMES (December 1984): 51.

Lunardini, Christine. ANTIC, THE ATARI RESOURCE (January 1985): 81-82.

The' Lee. PERSONAL SOFTWARE (July 1984): 80.

PROGRAM TITLE: REVOLUTIONS: PAST, PRESENT, AND FUTUTRE

GRADE LEVEL: 7 and up   GROUP: individual or small

PUBLISHER: Focus Media, Inc.
           839 Stewart Ave.
           Garden City, NY 11530
           (516) 794-8900

SYSTEM REQUIREMENTS: Apple II+, IIe, or IIc/disk drive/48K

PACKAGE INCLUDES: 5 program diskettes, instructor's manual (44 pp.)

INSTRUCTIONAL MODE: tutorial, drill and practice

SUBJECT: political science, world history

COMMENTS: A comprehensive program that employs the computer's graphics mode in teaching about the American, French, and Russian revolutions. It also permits an analysis of the likelihood of future revolutions given criteria established from an examination of the three historical models. The content is accurate and provides for in-depth coverage on the topic. The instructor's manual is excellent. It includes suggested lesson plans for a unit as well as an extensive bibliography.

PROGRAM TITLE: RUN FOR THE MONEY

GRADE LEVEL: 10 and up   GROUP: individual or pairs

PUBLISHER: Scarborough Systems, Inc.
           25 North Broadway
           Tarrytown, NY 10591
           (800) 882-8882

SYSTEM REQUIREMENTS: Apple II+, IIe, or IIc/48K/disk drive/Compiled BASIC

Atari 400, 800, or XL series/32K/disk drive/Compiled BASIC

Commodore 64/disk drive/ Compiled BASIC

IBM PC, XT, or jr/64K/disk drive/Compiled BASIC

Macintosh/128K/disk drive/Compiled BASIC

PACKAGE INCLUDES: 1 diskette, instruction manual
(32 pp.), command card

INSTRUCTIONAL MODE: simulation, educational game

SUBJECT: economics, future travel

COMMENTS: Designed for three levels of play
(beginner, expert, and tycoon), this game teaches
basic principles of the free enterprise system such
as supply and demand, advertising, and the role of
competition. Students simulate a forced landing by
a space ship. The object is to create sufficient
profit to purchase the necessary protective paint
to complete the return journey. The complexity of
the program necessitates genuine concentration on
the part of the players. The manual is well written
and there is an on-screen tutorial to add to one's
understanding of the game and its strategies.

ADDITIONAL REVIEWS: Battaglini, Raymond. COMPUTE
(March 1985): 76-77.

Casey J.M. CLASSROOM COMPUTER LEARNING 5 (February
1985): 14.

Keogh, Jim. PERSONAL SOFTWARE (June 1984): 70.

Lechner, Jack. GAMES (December 1984): 51.

Monahan, C. CUE NEWSLETTER (November 1984): 27.

Wiswell, Phil. PC MAGAZINE (July 10, 1984):
291-292.

PROGRAM TITLE: SIMPOLICON

GRADE LEVEL: 9 - college   GROUP: individual,
small, or class

PUBLISHER: Cross Cultural Software
5385 Elrose Avenue
San Jose, CA 95724
(408) 267-1044

SYSTEM REQUIREMENTS: Apple II, II+, IIe, or
IIc/48K/2 disk drives/ Applesoft BASIC

PACKAGE INCLUDES: 1 program diskette (with backup),
1 country data diskette, and 1 instruction manual
(100 pp.)

INSTRUCTIONAL MODE: simulation

SUBJECT: economics, global studies

COMMENTS: This realistic portrayal of the complex
process and problems of national economic
development is sophisticated, yet it raises some
basic economic questions. Students must create and
maintain a stable, secure country with a balanced
economy. In the process, the students must ask
questions about how to allocate resources such as
agricultural land and mineral deposits. Similarly,
players must determine how to provide basic
societal needs such as education, health, and
distribution of goods and services. The
accompanying manual is excellent and contains many
useful activities.

ADDITIONAL REVIEWS: Brady, Holly. CLASSROOM
COMPUTER LEARNING (January 1985): 23-24.

PROGRAM TITLE: SOCIAL STUDIES - VOL. 2

GRADE LEVEL: 4-12   GROUP: individual or small

PUBLISHER: MECC
3490 Lexington Avenue North
St. Paul, MN 55112
(612) 481-3500

SYSTEM REQUIREMENTS: Apple II, II+, IIe, or
IIc/48K/disk drive/Applesoft BASIC

PACKAGE INCLUDES: 1 diskette (with backup), teacher's guide (88 pp.)

INSTRUCTIONAL MODE: drill and practice, tutorial, simulation, problem solving

SUBJECT: global studies, conflict resolution, economics

COMMENTS: Seven programs are included. BARGAIN, as its name implies, involves collective bargaining. Identifying capitals is the purpose of COUNTRY. International conflict is examined in CRISES. FAIL SAFE explores decision making on the presidential level. MINING involves information retrieval using agricultural data. STATES deals with capitals and geographic shape recognition. The directions for the programs are clearly stated. Thinking skills such as logic, memory, and synthesis are developed. Some graphics are difficult to read, and the length of display time for some screens is excessive.

PROGRAM TITLE: SOCIAL STUDIES - VOL. 6

GRADE LEVEL: 4-8   GROUP: individual or small

PUBLISHER: MECC
            3490 Lexington Avenue North
            St. Paul, MN 55112
            (612) 481-3500

SYSTEM REQUIREMENTS: Apple II, II+, IIe, or IIc/48K/disk drive/Applesoft BASIC

Atari 400, 800, 600XL, 800XL, or 1200X1/48K/disk drive/BASIC

Commodore 64/disk drive/BASIC

TRS-80 Model III or IV/48K/disk drive/BASIC

PACKAGE INCLUDES: 1 diskette, 1 back-up diskette, teacher's guide (81 pp.)

INSTRUCTIONAL MODE: simulation, drill and practice, tutorial, problem solving, and educational game

SUBJECT: history

COMMENTS: The package contains five programs.
VOYAGEUR and FURS simulate a fur trading
expedition. NOMAD gives the player a city map with
the task of finding an intersection. OREGON is a
simulation of a trip along the famous Oregon Trail.
SUMERIA simulates buying, selling, and planting in
an ancient society. The background information and
learning activities provided in the study guide are
excellent for additional learning. Effective
graphics and motivational activites such as the
"hunt" in OREGON are typical drill and practice
uses of the computer's capabilities. The background
music in OREGON and VOYAGEUR, however, could be a
distraction in the classroom if other
teaching/learning activities are taking place.

ADDITIONAL REVIEWS: Muir, S.P. CHIME (February
1983): 4-5.

Page, Marilyn. MICROCOMPUTERS IN EDUCATION (October
1983): 5.

Tennis, Jean. TEACHING AND COMPUTERS (Spring 1983):
31-32.

White, C.S. SOCIAL EDUCATION 47 (May 1983):
338-339.

PROGRAM TITLE: TRAIL WEST

GRADE LEVEL: elementary and up   GROUP: individual
or small

PUBLISHER: Micro-Ed, Inc.
           Box 444005
           Eden Prarie, MN 55344
           (800) 642-7633

SYSTEM REQUIREMENTS: Commodore 64/disk drive or
cassette recorder/BASIC

PET/8K/disk drive or cassette recorder/BASIC

TI 99/4A/16K/cassette recorder/BASIC

VIC-20/3.5K/cassette recorder/BASIC

PACKAGE INCLUDES: 1 diskette or 1 cassette, instructions

INSTRUCTIONAL MODE: educational game or simulation

SUBJECT: U.S. history (California)

COMMENTS: This simulation gives players an opportunity to experience some of the hardships faced by those who participated in the "Gold Rush" to California in the 1850's. At the outset, each player receives certain amounts of food, ammunition, and other necessities to make a two-thousand mile trip. The object is to apportion these goods so they will last until the end of the journey. The program has proved too difficult for most primary level children. The graphics are interesting and appropriate. The program offers limited practice with compass directions and coordinate graphing.

PROGRAM TITLE: U.S. CONSTITUTION TUTOR

GRADE LEVEL: 7-12   GROUP: individual or small

PUBLISHER: Micro lab, Inc.
           Skokie Valley Road
           Highland Park, IL 60035
           (312) 433-7550

SYSTEM REQUIREMENTS: Apple II+ or IIe/48K/disk drive/Applesoft BASIC

Commodore 64/disk drive/BASIC

IBM PC or jr/64K/disk drive/BASIC

PACKAGE INCLUDES: 1 diskette (user can make backup), instruction manual (50 pp.)

INSTRUCTIONAL MODE: tutorial, drill and practice

SUBJECT: United States - constitutional law

COMMENTS: The program is intended for junior high and senior high school students and adults who are taking citizenship tests. It covers the three branches of government and other topics typically dealt with, such as separation of powers, checks and balances, and federal vs. state jurisdiction. The content of the program is sound, but the wait time between questions seems unreasonably long. This is unfortunate because it makes what is otherwise a superior program tedious and lackluster.

ADDITIONAL REVIEWS: Cefaloni, Don. POLITICAL SCIENCE MICRO REVIEW (May 1983): 45-47.

Green, Denise. INFOWORLD 5 (September 12, 1983): 37, 52-53.

PROGRAM TITLE: UNLOCKING THE MAP CODE

GRADE LEVEL: 4-6 GROUP: individual or small

PUBLISHER: Rand McNally and Company
          8255 North Central Park Avenue
          Skokie, IL 60076
          (312) 673-9100

SYSTEM REQUIREMENTS: Apple IIe or IIc/64K/disk drive/color monitor/FORTH

Atari 400 or 800/48K/disk drive/color monitor/FORTH

PACKAGE INCLUDES: 2 diskettes, teacher's guide (13 pp.), students' workbook (18 pp.)

INSTRUCTIONAL MODE: tutorial, drill and practice

SUBJECT: geography

COMMENTS: Program fosters six map and globe skills: land and water forms, interpreting color and map symbols, directions, location, scale, and time. Most of the units involve the students in interactive, meaningful, and motivating work. The documentation is outstanding, with complete descriptions for each unit. Graphics are

effectively used to illustrate and drill students
on difficult concepts. The progoram has two minor
shortcomings. First, much of the learning relies
heavily on worksheet exercises. These must be
completed at the computer and do not facilitate
effective use of computer time. Second, information
is entered by the space bar rather than the return
key.

ADDITIONAL REVIEWS: Watson, Nancy, and James
Watson. ELECTRONIC LEARNING (May/June 1984): 97.

PROGRAM TITLE: WHERE IN THE WORLD IS CARMEN
SANDIEGO?

GRADE LEVEL: 5 and up   GROUP: individual or small

PUBLISHER: Broderbund
           17 Paul Drive
           San Rafael, CA 94903-2101
           (415) 479-1170

SYSTEM REQUIREMENTS: Apple II+, IIe, or IIc/disk
drive/64K/joystick optional

PACKAGE INCLUDES: 1 diskette (90 day full warranty
and limited warranty thereafter), documentation (16
pp.), The World Almanac and Book of Facts

INSTRUCTIONAL MODE: game

SUBJECT: world geography

COMMENTS: Placed in the role of being a detective,
the player can advance in rank from rookie to ace
while pursuing international criminals. A variety
of clues can help the player identify which of the
ten criminals is being pursued by using the police
dossiers that are provided; one of the crime
figures is the source of the title of the program.
The World Almanac helps the player unravel the
clues that are generated from the program. A fun
game that can promote learning basic facts about
various cities around the world while sharpening
problem-solving skills.

CHAPTER 5

MANAGING INSTRUCTION

WITH COMPUTERS

The home, the workplace, and institutional settings
such as the school are where computers are most
frequently found. In each of these domains the
computer's versatility is employed to perform
several functions. Among the tasks that computers
can handle are: word processing, managing
databases, producing graphics, and displaying
electronic spreadsheets. Our society is
experiencing the emergence of what some futurists
call an "Information Age." By this they mean that
we are entering a period of time that will be
characterized by the unique ways we generate,
access, and process information (Petofi, 1985).
     The ability to use a computer will become a
prerequisite for many careers. Furthermore, this
need will spread throughout the various of roles
within an organization. For example, at higher and
higher levels of responsibility, in middle and
upper level management, computer skills such as
word processing and database management are
becoming part of the qualifications for such
positions. In addition to using computers for
teaching purposes, schools at both the elementary
and secondary levels will feel increasing pressure
to revise curriculum to include the teaching to
students of computers skills described as
information processing. Social studies is a subject
area that is ideal for providing learning
activities that are centered around information
processing tasks. Examples of these tasks are
managing data, preparing graphic displays of
information, and preparing reports and charts.
     According to Ragsdale (1982), educational
software can be subdivided into two types: that
which is designed to help us "teach through
computers" and that which is designed to help us to
"teach with computers." Chapters 3 and 4 emphasize
the former type of computer use: directly providing

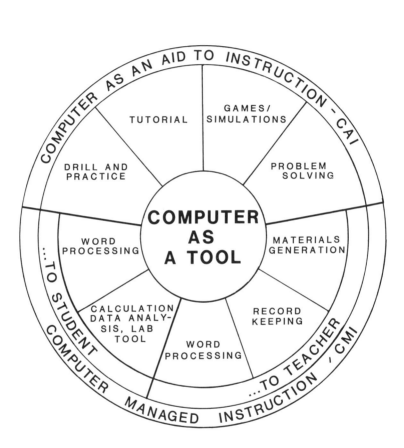

instruction to the student. When used for this
purpose, to assist in providing instruction, the
computer and accompanying software are referred to
as Computer Assisted Instruction (CAI). The
application of the computer to traditional teacher
tasks such as grade keeping, producing educational
activities, generating test items, or assessing
readability levels, are referred to as Computer
Managed Instruction (CMI). In addition, any use of
the computer in an educational activity such as the
use of a word processor to write a report or
accessing a database as part of a research project
will also be considered CMI. Table 5.1 graphically
displays the roles and relationships of the various
CAI and CMI software to the social studies.

     This chapter examines additional ways for both
the teacher and student to use the computer for
information processing. Thus, students will acquire
skills that they can use in learning about social
studies that will continue to be of value to them
as our culture moves through the "Information
Age."

DATABASES: WHAT ARE THEY?

     Computerized databases refer to the use of
software for the purpose of storing and cataloging
information. Before the development of the
computer, however, non-computerized databases
existed. Examples of non-computerized databases
that you are already familiar with are the card
catalog in a library or a recipe box. In each of
these examples information is stored in an orderly
fashion. In the case of the card catalog
information is stored by author, title, or subject.
In a recipe box, a cook could sort according to
dish (entree, salad, vegetable, or dessert),
country of recipe origin, ingredients, or
alphabetically. Unfortunately, when using
non-computerized databases the storage, retrieval,
and modification of data had to be performed
laboriously by hand.

     Computers offer a tremendous advantage in the
management of databases because of the amazing
speed with which a computer can simultaneously
isolate and retrieve several variables from a
database. For example, if a computerized version of
a recipe file were created, each entry or file

could include the previously mentioned descriptors
of dish, country of recipe origin, or ingredients.
If the user wanted all French breakfast dishes that
contained onions these descriptors can be given to
the computer which will then search the entire
database retrieving only those files that meet the
criteria of the descriptors. Additional advantages
of the computer are the large amounts of
information that can be stored in a relatively
compact arrangement on either a floppy or hard
disk. Through telephone lines it is possible to
have different types of computers interact. Thus, a
large and powerful mainframe, which may store
hundreds of extensive databases, can be available
to the operator of a microcomputer through a
patchwork of special pieces of equipment that will
permit the computers to communicate with each
other. Before describing in more detail how a
mainframe and microcomputer can be linked together,
what follows is a description of the origin and
different types of databases available.

In the late 1950's databases were developed as
an alternative to purchasing an expensive
mainframe. In these pre microchip days, many
companies desired the services of a computer but
could not afford the expense involved to purchase
one. Thus, companies sprang up whose sole purpose
was to acquire a mainframe and then through "time
sharing" offer computer time to those firms unable
to purchase their own mainframe but who still
wanted to access the database.

Special equipment was needed in order to take
advantage of "time sharing" a mainframe. That
equipment evolved into the delivery mechanisms we
have available now. Today's well-developed system
is possible because sophisticated computers are
available, specialized software has been developed,
standards and protocols established, and electronic
packet switching networks arranged. The computer
peripherals that have facilitated the reliable
transfer of information from one computer to
another represent the technology that has heralded
the Information Age.

The evolution of the microcomputer brought the
cost of time sharing to such an affordable level
that large numbers of private companies and
individuals invested in brokers who offered time
sharing to their accounts. The result was a

meteoric rise in the electronic information
industry. Today there are more than 1350 different
commercial computerized "databases." Additionally,
there are approximately 450 free, computerized
bulletin board and message exchange systems. All of
this is available through a telephone call placed
with the aid of relatively inexpensive peripheral
computer equipment and specialized software.

Databases have been classified into seven
different types (Glossbrenner, 1983). While these
classifications may be imperfect, they do offer the
reader an idea of the scope of databases that are
available. Glossbrenner's classification of
databases includes the following:

information utilities
encyclopedic database
news and specialized information databases
free computer bulletin board systems
electronic shopping, banking, and barter
computerized conferencing
telecommuting

The first two types of databases to be
discussed are actually quite similar. Information
utilities is a term coined to describe a database
that offers both information and services. These
databases don't require professional expertise and
can easily be used by the average person. They
offer a variety of information on a wide range of
topics. In addition to being an information source,
the information utilities also offer services such
as electronic mailing and shopping. Encyclopedic
databases offer access to information similar to
what is contained in the utilities. The difference
is that encyclopedic databases go into much more
depth and do not offer services such as electronic
mailing. A revolutionary development in the area of
information utilities designed specifically for
education, which should become available in many
classrooms during the next five years, is described
in the Afterword.

The remaining five classifications of
databases should also be of interest to social
studies teachers. Among these are the News and
Specialized Business Information Databases which
includes a service, the New York Times Information

Service (NYTIS) that provides the entire text of the New York Times. Each of the hundreds of Free Computer Bulletin Board Systems (CBBSs) on-line today offer feature articles written by contributors to the system as well as informational items and tips on using various hardware and software packages. Electronic shopping, banking, and barter databases are, as their name implies, a way to sit at home and browse through the descriptions and prices of over 50,000 items, everything from Izod shirts to Cross pen and pencil sets. As was explained earlier, some of these same services are available through some of the information utilities. Computerized conferencing and telecommuting are ways of networking workers to facilitate organizational communication. For example, three individuals in different locations can offer suggestions to each other via the computer. Telecommuting is the rapidly growing phenomenon whereby individuals perform their work functions in their own home with the aid of a personal computer.

The ERIC clearinghouse for social studies education has compiled a synopsis of fourteen databases available to social studies teachers which can be found in Appendix B. Also included in Appendix B are sample citations from four social studies related databases as well as a description of how social studies teachers can access the entire ERIC collection through a personal computer. Readers interested in obtaining more information about what is available through ERIC should contact the ERIC Clearinghouse in Boulder, Colorado. In addition to supplying detailed information about databases, ERIC also provides step by step instructions for conducting a search using ERIC.

ACCESSING DATABASES

For a cost ranging between $300 and $1200 one can equip the typical microcomputer found in a social studies classroom with the following computer peripherals:

        A plug-in communications card
        A device called a "modem"
        A cable to connect the two
        A communications software package

A telephone

By acquiring this equipment and accompanying software, the user can have access, usually for a fee, to an amazing wealth of information. The variance in cost of the equipment and software is dependent on the particular configuration of peripherals chosen. The more expensive equipment will have more versatility and sophistication than the lesser priced products. The buyer should be prepared to shop around as computer dealers and manufacturers will frequently put these items on sale.

Actual access to most databases is controlled by brokers who charge a fee for using their services. Like the cost for equipment, the broker's charge will also vary. Usually there is an initial one-time only connect charge of approximately $100 and then a charge, often approximately $9 an hour during the evening hours, for the connect time used when the two computers communicate. A well-defined search of the database can keep this connect time to somewhere around two minutes per search. Thus, much of the expense involved in using databases is for equipment and for covering such brokerage needs as registration, account setup, etc. If the user is well acquainted with designing the search, the actual on-going expense of connect time between the computers is negligible in comparison to the vast amounts of information available to the user. Following is a description of how this communication between computers over telephone lines is possible.

As you may recall from Chapter Two, the microcomputer stores and processes information in the form of binary notation with eight bits, or a multiple, to the byte. There are two types of cables through which bytes can be processed the computer, parallel, when all eight bits travel in unison, or serial, when each bit is sent one at a time.A telephone line, the medium through which a microcomputer can access a database stored on a mainframe, can only handle one bit at a time. The function of the communication card, which is plugged into one of the peripheral slots in the back of the motherboard, is to recode the data so that all information is in serial form since that is the only way the information can be transmitted over phone lines. The communication card, then forwards the serial information to the second step in the communication link, the modem.

Modems come in two types: "acoustic couplers" and "direct connect." A direct connect modem has the advantage of sending its frequencies directly through telephone lines since it plugs into the commonplace modular jack. An acoustic coupler is a headset which uses any phone receiver and is independent of the type of phone jack. The disadvantage of the acoustic coupler is the necessity of having a good connection so the proper frequency can be transmitted. Regardless of the type of modem used, it will perform the same function which is to modulate the digital signals of the computer into sound waves. The modem can also demodulate the sounds that are transmitted through phone lines into digital bits which the computer can use. The word modem is derived from the first syllables of the two words that describe its function, MODulation and DEMomdulation.

The final function of equipment in a computing system that employs a modem is the communication software. As with the other components that have been described, the cost of this software will range from $25 to $150. Similarly, the more expensive price reflects additional features and is usually easier to use. Essentially, communication software instructs your computer how to process information so it can be sent and received as well as playing a role in establishing and maintaining a connection with another system. In a sense, communication software creates an illusion that the user's terminal is a "dumb terminal." In the parlance of the computer world, this refers to the fact that the user's system is serving only to send and receive information from another system.

The notion of a dumb terminal is an important concept. Assuming the user has carefully investigated the compatibility of equipment, not only can a microcomputer user communicate with a mainframe system, it is also possible for two microcomputers to be in communication. For example, if I am at home and am using a computer to enter student grades for an assignment, I can send and store the information to a computer at my school, provided the necessary equipment is in operation. Once the novice is exposed to the process, it

A modem is the equipment that provides a computer user with access to databases by accessing telephone lines. (Photo courtesy of Apple Computer, Inc.)

becomes almost as simple as dialing a telephone. In
fact, that is essentially what the user is doing
through the software and the modem, employing the
computer as a telephone. As the movie WAR GAMES
depicted and newspaper stories about teenage
"hackers" have pointed out, the steps in accessing
a mainframe through a communication system attached
to microcomputer can be learned by very young
students. Rather than place temptation in the path
of an aspiring student, the social studies teacher
should closely monitor those who have access to the
various codes and procedural protocols of any
databases used in classroom activities. Otherwise,
at the end of the month there might be a hefty
connect time bill because an eager student spent
hours at home working with a database account
issued to a teacher.

     An excellent example of the use of computers
and telecommunications for social studies is
available through the University of Michigan. They
have developed a complex simulation titled
"Arab-Israeli Exercise." It is a sophisticated and
exemplary use of the technology. For more details
the reader is referred to annotated bibliography at
the end of Chapter 7 (see Interactive
Communications Simulation).

SOFTWARE FOR CREATING YOUR OWN DATABASE

     All previous discussion about accessing
mainframe databases through computer communication
equipment assumes that there will be sufficient
money available in the school budget to purchase
the equipment and establish an account. Given the
restricted funding available to the majority of
school systems today, this may not be the case. The
above discussion was included because there is
always the hope that funding for education will
improve, and in some wealthier districts, adequate
money for these types of experiences is available.
Until then, the social studies teacher has three
options. First, find alternative sources of
funding. For example, one teacher, who owned her
own equipment and account, had students write
searches which she then conducted at home during
the evenings. The students took up collections to
cover the minor connect charge of $9.00 a month.
     There remain two options to which social

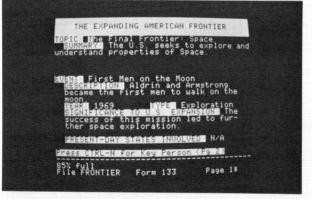

ABOVE: Scholastic Software's exclusive educational versions of PFS:
WRITE, PFS:FILE and PFS:REPORT. In addition, Scholastic is publishing
four curriculum Data Files (above: screen shot from U.S. History Data
File) for use with PFS:FILE and PFS:REPORT. For middle grades through
college level; Apple and IBM. CONTACT: Avery Hunt, Communications,
Scholastic, 212/505-3410.

The Scholastic family of PFS programs and an example of a
file from PFS: File. (Photo courtesy Scholastic, Inc.)

studies teacher can turn in their desire to help
students acquire information processing skills and
familiarity with databases. The first is to
purchase a software package that contains a
publisher created database. The second option is to
purchase software the teacher, or students, could
use to create their own database. Programs such as
these have recently been developed and the
following will describe in more detail what is
involved in creating, or using a preexisting,
database.

Rather than reinventing the wheel, Scholastic,
Inc., has taken a popular and user friendly
database program known as PFS, which is an acronym
for Personal Filing System, and adapted it for use
in social studies classes. The Scholastic PFS
family of databased software is designed for
students and teachers from fifth grade and up who
have had a range of experience, from very limited
to extensive, using computers. Five programs make
up the social studies package. The software is
compatible with Apple IIe, IIc/ disk drive/ 64K.
There is also a version for the IBM PC, PCjr/ disk
drive/ 128K. For either version both a printer and
a second disk drive are recommended.

The mainstay of the Scholastic PFS
constellation of software is Scholastic PFS:File
that can store and retrieve a vast array of
information in a format created by the user.
Scholastic PFS:Report is a support program that can
be used to create tables to present information the
user selects from File. Scholastic PFS:Write is, as
its name suggests, a word processing program which
can also insert data from File in the composition
of documents.

The final two programs, Scholastic U.S.
History and U.S. Government, are preexisting
databases covering a wide range of topics.
Scholastic has plans to develop a geography
database. It should be noted that the preexisting
databases can only be used with the File program.
Other publishers are also beginning to develop and
market preexisting databases that are compatible
with Scholastic PFS:File, Report, and Write. (For
more information see the annotated bibliography in
Chapter 6.)

The Scholastic:PFS programs are the first of
their kind on the market and are a major

breakthrough for the social studies teacher who has
been looking for a way to help students acquire
research skills while taking advantage of the
computer's potential as a vehicle for learning.
Research skills such as discovering commonalities
and differences among groups of events and
variables, analyzing relationships, identifying
trends, testing and refining hypotheses
are a few examples of the learning that students
encounter when they work with Report, File, and the
two preexisting databases, U.S. History and U.S.
Government. Of course, the Write program is a boon
to the teacher who accepts the responsibility for
teaching reading and writing concurrently with
social studies content.

The Scholastic PFS:File package contains two
file disks, two sample data files called Books, and
an accompanying handbook that is an extensive and
exceptionally well-prepared guide for teaching and
learning about the program and its capabilities. In
fact, the documentation and learning activities
included in the handbook are exemplary in the area
of computer curriculum development. The handbook is
divided into six sections, the first being an
overview and guideline for using the manual.

Section two of the File handbook is the
teaching guide that explains why teachers and
students would find these programs useful in
handling multiple pieces of information. Also
included in this section are guidelines for
preparing teachers and students for using the
package in the classroom. Classroom management
suggestions, based on the number of computers
available for students, are given. A scope and
sequence chart outlines which activities are
designed to teach specific skills. The skills fall
under the general categories of retrieving
information, designing files, building files, and
preparing reports. Strategies for introducing and
managing the learning activities are provided. The
section concludes with plans for assessing student
progress and meeting individual needs.

Complete details on all the functions and
features of the program are included in the
Reference Guide section of the the handbook. It
contains the step-by-step procedures for
accomplishing particular tasks such as saving data
in a file. Immediately following this is the

Mini-Reference Guide section which is handy for
those who are familiar with the program and need a
quick reference for the steps involved in
performing a particular task.

The Learning Activities section contains
self-study materials. These take the learner,
either teacher or student, step by step through the
concepts and skills of using both File and its
support program Report. Report offers the user a
self-explanatory guide for organizing information
from File into tabular form. It should be noted
that File can be run independently of Report, but
the converse is not true. Fourteen learning
activities, each requiring 15 minutes to complete,
have been written for those with a sixth-grade or
better reading level. The learning activities teach
concepts and skills such as categorizing,
cross-referencing, alphabetizing, designing files,
gathering data for student created files, and
preparing reports of the files. The final two
sections of the handbook contain reference cards, a
glossary, and appendices.

As was described previously, Scholastic
PFS:Report is a support program intended for use
with File. Report offers the user first-hand
experience with using the computer to attain a goal
of social studies instruction, constructing and
interpreting tables of information. The Report
package is identical to the File package with the
following exceptions. Report has its own program
disk and a disk called Sortwork and unlike File,
the computing system must include two disk drives.
The manual contains the same sections as File with
the exception that the Learning Activities section
for Reports is included in the File manual only.

The publisher created databases are useful
sources of information that the teacher can use for
a variety of purposes. A Scope and Sequence chart
from U.S. History is shown in figure 5.2. It gives
the reader an idea of the potential the Scholastic
PFS software holds for teaching students concepts
and computer skills simultaneously. Included in the
U.S. History database are files covering such
topics as the Frontier, Inventions, 20th Century,
and Presidents. Each of these files contains an
average of 140 entries with three pages, also
called screens, of information for each entry.
About 80% of the available memory for each file has

been used for data storage. Thus, the users can add
a considerable amount of information of their own
for each topic. Additionally, U.S. History has two
files that contain only descriptors and the users
must enter their own data. These files are titled
Local History and Fun. The former title represents
an area of study that should be developed at the
elementary and middle levels of the social studies
curriculum. The latter title is a file that should
more properly be designated "twentieth-century
trivia." Nonetheless it is an enjoyable unit to
work with that reinforces PFS skills and concepts
previously introduced.

The second publisher created database in the
Scholastic PFS family is U.S. Government. As with
the U.S. History database there are several files
and accompanying teaching units that have been
created by the publisher. There are also two files,
Local Government and State Government, whose
descriptors have been provided by the publisher but
require student input of data. Included in the
files of the Scholastic PFS:U.S. Government
database are the following: elections, federal
spending, and constitutional convention.

Both the teaching units and the data files of
U.S. Government, and the companion program U.S.
History, do not assume a high level of content
expertise by the user. Readability is estimated at
a sixth-grade level, and thus the packages have
been designed to accommodate a wide range of ages
and skills. The activities have been
developmentally organized so younger students may
not be able complete all the activities in a unit
while older students may progress quickly to the
more advanced, open-ended activities found at the
unit's conclusion. Both guides include the
following sections: teaching guide, publisher
created files, student created files, quick guide,
mini-references for File and Report, and a
glossary/appendix.

As was mentioned previously, other publishers
are developing preexisting databases that are
compatible with the Scholastic PFS programs. While
packaged somewhat differently, they are nontheless
easy to use and provide a rich source of learning.
(Specific information can be found in Chapter 6:
annotated bibliorgraphy entry, "Social Studies Fact
Finder.")

Fun With American History ♠

I = Skill Introduced
P = Skill Practiced

Skills	Activity									
	1	2	3	4	5	6	7	8	9	10
Discover the main topics, key events, important people, and trends within a period of history	I	P			P	P	P	P		
Classify data into relevant categories	I	P			P	P	P	P		
Note cause-and-effect relationships	I	P			P	P	P	P		
Define a historical problem or question	I	P			P	P		P		
Identify data needed to answer a historical question	I	P			P	P		P		
Use library references, including card catalogs, almanacs, government publications, and books	I	P	P				P	P		
Sequence and organize data needed to answer a historical question		I			P	P		P		
Analyze and interpret results of the data collected						I		P		
Present a synthesis of research selecting from several formats (graph, chart, or print)						I		P		
Validate data collected to ensure objectivity, technical correctness, and currency			I				P	P		
Estimate the adequacy of information collected			I			P	P	P		
Discuss implications of research and propose additional hypotheses						I				
Propose a course of action based on research results								I		
Operate a computer to enter and retrieve information from a variety of sources				I	P	P	P	P		
Use computer information networks								I		

A scope and sequence chart from Scholastic PFS.
(Reprinted with permission from Scholastic, Inc.)

The final piece in the Scholastic PFS package is a word processing program that will be discussed later in this chapter. Overall, the Scholastic version of PFS is a hallmark in the development of computerized curriculum materials for social studies educators. It is comprehensive and thorough in its coverage of topics. The guides, which are really documentation written for teachers, are clear and easy to follow. The illustrations and information the guide contains should help demystify the computer and its social studies applications for even the most reluctant teacher. While there are other data management programs available, none of the documentation has been adapted for teacher/student use to the extent that Scholastic has modified PFS. One minor criticism regarding the documentation is that the illustrations exclude figures representing minorities. Before we leave the topic of data management there is one additional program that is part of the PFS family which is worth highlighting.

PFS:Graph is one member of the family of software that has not yet been modified by Scholastic. Nonetheless, it is an important piece of software for the social studies teacher using File or the two preexisting databases, U.S. Government and U.S. History. Thus, PFS:Graph is completely compatible with the Scholastic versions even though the documentation looks different. With Graph the user can take the information from a file and reproduce it as a line, bar, or pie graph. While the documentation for Graph is different than the Scholastic PFS family, it is still quite comprehensible and relatively easy to learn and teach students how to use.

GUIDELINES FOR CREATING A DATABASE

Social studies teachers should realize that students will profit from close guidance in using databases. Guidance is particularly important as students learn how to develop categories of information; sometimes these are referred to as fields. The work of Hilda Taba (1967), a recognized theorist and researcher in social studies, is an excellent resource for guiding students' thinking skills in regard to concept development and interpretation of data. A critical task faced by the teacher, then, is to help the students list, group, explain, label, and regroup information. The second critical task is to assist children interpret the data. Of course, a program such as Scholastic PFS:Reports can be of immense help to students as they arrange and organize the data developed during the concept development phase.

While Taba did not forsee the microcomputer as a revolutionary tool in managing databases, she would readily agree that it does not in any way diminish the role of the social studies teacher. Helping students group information, identify fields, and rearrange these categories as needed is still a central function of the teacher. Similarly, the interpretation of data including analyzing relationships, identifying cause and effect, comparing and contrasting data, drawing conclusions, and reconsidering all previous steps requires teacher guidance and sequential development of student skills. The social studies teacher who assumes that students already have certain skills and experiences regarding databases will take only minimal advantage of the computer's potential. Careful guidance is necessary.

WORD PROCESSING PROGRAMS AND OTHER WAYS COMPUTERS HANDLE INFORMATION

The art of composition is in the process of technological transformation thanks to software known as word processing. With the aid of a word processing program one of the most important and tedious aspects of writing, revision, becomes a relatively easy task. Pencil and paper and the typewriter represent physical barriers to most writers when it comes to revision since they must reproduce the entire document to incorporate any emendations. As far as actually encoding thought onto paper, the computer really functions no differently than a typewriter. However, if an author thinks a different word, or a correction of any sort, is necessary it is simply a matter of using the edit function of the software to make any changes. The edit function of most word processing programs will permit the user to make any number of changes such as rearranging paragraphs, rewording sentences, or correcting spelling with a few key

strokes. The writer is thus free to concentrate on
exploring the flexibility and power of language
without the burden of producing a perfect first
draft. Word processing gives the author a sense of
unbridled freedom to compose since whatever is
encoded can so easily be changed.

While there are a variety of excellent word
processing programs available for both teachers and
students, we will examine Scholastic PFS:Write
since the reader is already familiar with the other
programs in this family. The manual that
accompanies Scholastic PFS:Write gives the user
three options for learning how to use the program.
Two of these options are experiential and involve
the learner in working at the keyboard as they work
through the manual; the third requires the user to
become familiar with the content in the reference
guide section of the manual prior to working at the
keyboard. In addition, the manual has the same
sections as the other Scholastic PFS programs:
introduction, teaching guide, mini-reference,
learning activities, and glossary. The manual and
learning activities are an excellent resource for
either teacher or student to gain a sense of
mastery over word processing capabilities by
becoming familiar with PFS:Write.

As is typical of most word processing
programs, Scholastic PFS:Write can perform several
related tasks in producing a document. These
include encoding and editing which are used for
writing and revising respectively. One part of the
software helps the user design the format of the
page including margins, indentation, numeration,
and page headings or footings. The print function
lets the user determine intervals between lines,
continuous or single page feed, number of copies,
and the option of merging information from
PFS:Graph of PFS:File within a document. Finally,
files from the disk can be saved on other disks,
removed, or called into working memory with a few
key strokes. As word processing programs go (others
will highlighted in Chapter 6) Scholastic PFS:write
performs many of the functions commonly found. It
is a relatively easy program to learn. Its chief
disadvantage is a limited amount of memory
available to the user. That is, it is an excellent
program for composing letters and reports of under
ten pages. Other software programs, although more

An example of the AppleWorks spreadsheet. (Photo courtesy of Apple Computer, Inc.)

difficult to master, are more appropriate for a
writer composing extensive manuscripts.

In addition to word processing, computers can
also be used to create neatly arranged tables of
numbers similar to what an accountant might do with
an accounting sheet. This type of program is
referred to as an electronic spreadsheet and, as
the name implies, is a sheet created by the user
where information is spread out so as to be more
comprehensible. Some programs such as AppleWorks,
which is cited in Chapter 6, is interactive and can
combine its spreadsheet function with those of word
processing and data management. An interactive
database management software can permit the user to
produce documents based on files in each type of
program included in the package. Thus, students
could produce reports using the word processing
program and include tables and charts as
documentation with the spreadsheet program. A
bibliography could be included from the database
program of the package.

The concept of an electronic spreadsheet has
been modified for the educational software market
by publishers who appeal directly to teachers by
creating a grade keeping program. Programs
developed to directly help the teacher with tasks
such as creating crossword puzzles, recording
grades, or generating tests are most often referred
to as teacher utility programs. Most of these
programs are very easy to use but specific and
limited in the functions they perform. Thus, for
tasks such as grade keeping, teachers might as well
take the time to learn an interactive program
because they offer such versatility.

The final examples of CMI are lesson-authoring
systems and languages. These are two ways the
teacher can create a variety of individually
designed learning experiences employing any one of
the approaches used in CAI. Authoring systems are
in their infancy and require little or no previous
programming expertise. Authoring languages are more
flexible but require considerable study for the
user to become proficient in the command structure.
Authoring languages are often subsets of more
general programming languages. Chapter 6 is an
annotated bibliography that contains references for
authoring systems as well as word processing and
other teacher utility programs.

BIBLIOGRAPHY

Burke R.L. CAI SOURCEBOOK. Englewood Cliffs, N.J.:
Prentice-Hall, 1982.

An introduction into developing, writing, and
marketing CAI software. Provides step-by-step
instructions for writing with sample frame designs.
Includes information for validating CAI and
concludes with a look at the future of CAI and
microcomputing.

Butcher, Diane E. "On Line Searching: How to Get
Instant Information." ELECTRONIC LEARNING 2
(November/December 1984): 39-40.

Using an interview format, this article gives some
specific suggestions for conducting a literature
search. It begins by explaining what an information
system is and how to access information.
Highlighted are three on-line databases (Dialog,
BRS, and Orbit).

Edwards, Mary D. "Taking Electronic Field Trips in
Hawaii." ELECTRONIC LEARNING 2 (November/December
1984): 44.

Friedlander, Brian. "Get Your Class In-line and
On-line with a Modem." ELECTRONIC EDUCATION 5
(November/December 1985): 14-15.

A review of various databases and modems is
provided in this brief but informative article.
CompuServe, the Source, and DIALOG are among the
databases which are highlighted. Ten different
modems, their prices, and features are also
reviewed.

Glossbrenner, Alfred. THE COMPLETE HANDBOOK OF
PERSONAL COMPUTER COMMUNICATIONS: EVERYTHING YOU
NEED TO GO ONLINE WITH THE WORLD. New York: St.

Martin's Press, 1983.

An introduction to the world of telecommunications, the book provides a good background to the type of equipment needed to go on line. It also includes information on a wide variety of databses and how they can be accessed.

Hodges, J.O. "Using Database Management to Achieve Social Studies Objectives." VIRGINIA RESOLVES 27 (February 1985): 6-14.

Hunter, B. "The Case for a Classroom Database." INSTRUCTOR 94 (March 1985): 54-58.

Hunter, B. "Powerful Tools for Your Social Studies Classroom." CLASSROOM COMPUTER LEARNING (October 1983): 50-57.

Hunter, B. "Problem Solving with Databases." THE COMPUTING TEACHER 12 (May 1985): 20-27.

Jackson, Robert. "Five Ways to Use Databases in Social Studies." TEACHING AND COMPUTING 1 (January 1985): 16-20.

A brief look at various social studies, such as sociology, history, geography, career awareness, and global education, and how they can be used with databases. Provides minimal information about setting up a database.

Lesko, Matthew. THE COMPUTER DATA AND DATABASE SOURCE BOOK. New York: Avon Books, 1984.

A comprehensive collection of more than 1000 databases and necessary information for going on line with them. Includes annotated references which highlight the type of statistics or information contained for each entry.

McGinty, T. "Buying Modems: What to Look For." ELECTRONIC LEARNING 2 (November/December 1984): 42-43.

McKenzie, Jamieson A. "Computer Research for Social Studies." SOCIAL STUDIES TEACHER 6 (September/October 1984): 3.

Highlighted are the positive and negative aspects of computer research. For example, the question is raised regarding the potential of abuse of civil liberties by a party that conducts a computerized check of a citizen's library loans, or a check on credit card purchases. Also included are five basic skills the author suggests should be taught by social studies teachers for using databases.

Mecklenburger, J.A. "Looking Back to School." PHI DELTA KAPPAN 67 (October 1985): 119-122.

Nerby, Connie and Bob Hilgenfeld. "Using an Information Retrieval System in a Junior High School." THE COMPUTING TEACHER (January 1982): 53-54.

Parisi, Lynn. "Databases for Social Studies Education." Boulder, CO: ERIC Clearinghouse for Social Studies Education, 1984.

A number of publications are available for social studies teachers that are invaluable resources for using databases in classrooms. The types of databases that can be asccessed through the ERIC system are described including what they offer and fees that are charged. An excellent description of a sample search using ERIC is provided.

Petofi, Alexander. "Pixel Power: The Graphic Revolution in Computers." THE FUTURIST 19 (June 1985): 30-35.

Ragan, Andrew. "Marketing Your Own Software." ELECTRONIC LEARNING 2 (October 1984): 28-30

Useful advice is given for the individual or school district committee that desires to publish a piece of software that they have created. Included is a case study of a software development project. A list of publishers' addresses and some guidelines for how the market operates is also provided.

Ragsdale, R.G. COMPUTERS IN THE SCHOOLS: A GUIDE
FOR PLANNING. Ontario: Ontario Institute for
Studies in Education, 1982.

Riedesel, C. Alan, and Douglas H. Clements. COPING
WITH COMPUTERS IN THE ELEMENTARY AND MIDDLE
SCHOOLS. Englewood Cliffs, New Jersey:
Prentice-Hall, 1985.

A wide variety of topics are included in this
comprehensive look at using computers in schools,
ranging from computer literacy and social issues to
structuring early childhood experiences with
computers. The chapters end with thought-provoking
questions. The book is recommended as an
introductory text for pre-service and in-service
teachers. Two limitations are the brief, and highly
selective, reviews of software and the use of
questions rather than informative facts in the
annotated bibliography.

Rosenzweig, Laura. "Teaming up Social Studies and
Computer Teachers: A Geography Lesson that Combines
Databases and Computer Ethics." ELECTRONIC LEARNING
2 (April 1985): 16, 21.

A case is made for team teaching by instructors
whose specialties are computers and social studies.
An activity for combining a lesson on geography and
computer ethics is described. While no specific
recommendations are given, the lesson would be an
ideal adaptation of the PFS family that is
described in this chapter.

Taba, Hilda. "Implementing Thinking as an Objective
in Social Studies." In Jean Fair and Fannie R.
Shaftel, eds. EFFECTIVE THINKING IN THE SOCIAL
STUDIES. Washington, D.C.: National Council for the
Social Studies, 1967.

Tucker, S.A. "Selecting an Electronic Mail Service:
A Quest for the Holy Grail." DATABANK (February
1986): 86-101.

A comprehensive review of many electronic mail
services available and the types of equipment

needed are provided. The breakdown of features for
seven electronic mail services is   an excellent
resource.

White, C.S. "The Impact of Structured Activities
with a Computerized File Management Program on
Selected Information Processing Skills."
Unpublished Doctoral Dissertation. Indiana
University, Bloomington, Indiana, 1985.

This study involved more than 665 students who were
given information processing tasks involving the
manipulation of social studies data. The treatment
group had access to Scholastic PFS and the control
group did not. After controlling for variables such
as verbal ability, the researcher concluded that
"the results suggest that information-processing
skills can be enhanced through the use of
computerized file managment programs coupled with
structured activities."

White, C.S., and Allen D. Glenn. "Computers in the
Curriculum: Social Studies." ELECTRONIC LEARNING 2
(September 1984): 54-55.

CHAPTER 6

AN ANNOTATED BIBLIOGRAPHY OF

COMPUTER MANAGED

INSTRUCTIONAL SOFTWARE

As with the annotated bibliography of computer
assisted instruction, the following programs were
chosen because of their quality. In some cases, a
citation was entered because the software was the
only one that could perform a function for a
particular computer system. The bibliography is
comprehensive and citations include software that
will perform the following functions: database
management, word processing, spreadsheets, and
teacher utilities. The cost of the software is not
included in the reference because of frequent price
changes due to fluctuations in the software market.
Finally, the references and reviews cited in this
chapter should not be substituted for an in-depth
evaluation by the reader before purchasing any
program. The responsible social studies teacher
should be an informed decision maker when acquiring
either CAI or CMI software. This necessitates a
first-hand inquiry into cost benefits and cost
effectiveness before purchasing any software
(Mecklenburger, 1985).

PROGRAM TITLE: ALLWRITE

PUBLISHER: Prosoft
          P.O. Box 560
          North Hollywood, CA 91603
          (818) 764-3131

SYSTEM REQUIREMENTS: TRS-80 Model I, III, or
IV/48K/2 disk drives/Machine language

Compatible printer

PACKAGE INCLUDES: 1 diskette, documentation (338
pp.), 4 quick reference cards

FUNCTIONS: A general purpose word processing program.

COMMENTS: A simple program to use because its two key commands are based on the English language. In fact, the program is so easy that an experienced computer user could become comfortable with it in a very short time. In its ease of use, however, the designers have not neglected any functions one would expect for a top-of-the-line word processing program. In fact, the software will accommodate a wide range of compositions from form letters to long books.

ADDITIONAL REVIEWS: Kepner, Terry. 80 MICRO (November 1984): 35-36, 38.

PROGRAM TITLE: APPLE SUPERPILOT

PUBLISHER: Apple Computer, Inc.
         20525 Mariani Avenue
         Cupertino, CA 95014
         800-538-9696

SYSTEM REQUIREMENTS: Apple II, II+, IIe/48K/disk drives

PACKAGE INCLUDES: 4 diskettes (1 backup), documentation (312 pp.), editor's guide (178 pp.), Apple Co-Pilot

FUNCTIONS: An authoring language designed to give the teacher flexibility in creating CAI lessons for students.

COMMENTS: A powerful and flexible program that permits the classroom teacher to use a subset of Pascal, a general programming language. The advantage of using an authoring language is the relative ease and speed with which one can begin creating learning materials. Certain commands must be learned but the various editing sections of the program provide tutorial screens as well as easily accessed author tips. Teachers can create lessons incorporating such CAI features as sound, graphics, and text. Also under the control of the teacher is the sequencing of the material, answer matching, and classroom management functions. Individualized lessons can be created, but most teacher find Pilot more productive when used in groups to create curriculum where talents and skills can be pooled. Pilot could be used with students as a way of introducing them to elementary programming concepts.

ADDITIONAL REVIEWS: Beall, Sue. HEALTH EDUCATION MICROCOMPUTERS (October 1983): 94-95.

Furlong, M.S. SOCIAL EDUCATION 49 (January 1985): 59-62.

McKinnon, C.F. EDUCATIONAL TECHNOLOGY 22 (March 1982): 46.

Petersen, M. INFOWORLD 4 (November 15, 1982): 45-46.

Smith, Mike. CREATIVE COMPUTING 8 (July 1982): 62, 64, 67-68.

Volis, D.L. CLASSROOM COMPUTER NEWS 2 (March/April 1982): 53-54.

PROGRAM TILE: APPLEWORKS

PUBLISHER: Apple Computer, Inc.
           20525 Mariani Avenue
           Cupertino, CA 95014
           800-538-9696

SYSTEM REQUIREMENTS: Apple IIe or IIc/64K/disk drive/Assembly language 128K and 2 disk drives recommended

PACKAGE INCLUDES: Backup copies of the following can be made by the user: 1 two-sided boot and program diskette, 1 two-sided tutorial diskette, 1 sample file diskette, tutorial manual (150 pp.), and reference manual (300 pp.)

FUNCTIONS: An integrated software package that will perform the following functions: database

management, spreadsheet, and word processing
designed for general purposes.

COMMENTS: A relatively easy-to-use integrated
program that consists of a word processing,
spreadsheet, and filing system. The tutorial that
accompanies the package is very helpful and
provides a thorough step-by-step description of how
to use the system. The documentation is both well
written and a valuable source of information. The
program represents one of the best examples of its
kind on the market and could be used by social
studies teachers for filing, recording, and writing
reports about an individual student's progress. Or,
it could be applied to the process of developing
curriculum. Its value lies in its simplicity of
use, versatility of functions, and adaptability to
any number of teacher tasks. The teacher, however,
will have to make decisions about what can be
accomplished. In other words, the documentation,
while well written, is designed for the general
public and does not contain explicit ideas for
teachers.

ADDITIONAL REVIEWS: Anderson, Eric. BOOKLIST 81
(January 1, 1985): 652, 662-661.

Conklin, Joyce. CIDER PRESS (April 1984): 7.

Lundquist, Eric. BUSINESS COMPUTING SYSTEMS
(September 1, 1984): 128,130.

Schmeltz, L.R. NIBBLE (NOVEMBER 1984): 117-119.

Strehlo, Kevin. PERSONAL SOFTWARE (March 1984):
132-135, 162.

Tommervik, M.C. SOFTALK (April 1984): 121, 123.

Turner, Jack. THE COMPUTING TEACHER 12 (October
1984): 34-35.

PROGRAM TITLE: APPLE WRITER II

PUBLISHER: Apple Computer, Inc.
            20525 Mariani Avenue

Cupertino, CA 95014
408-996-1010

SYSTEM REQUIREMENTS: Apple II+, IIe, or
IIc/48K/disk drive/Assembley language/printer

PACKAGE INCLUDES: 1 diskette (with backup),
documentation (201 pp.)

FUNCTIONS: A general word processing program which
is designed to handle a wide variety of functions.

COMMENTS: A sophisticated word processing program
that allows the user to create, edit, format, and
print documents of all types. The documentation is
well written, but mastery of the commands takes a
considerable number of hours depending on the
user's familiarity with word processing and the
computer. The program has split screen capability
as well as a powerful feature called Word
Processing Language, which can be used to insert
frequently used phrases or paragraphs into
documents. The evolution of this program has made
it one of the best values on the market.

ADDITIONAL REVIEWS: Arrants, Stephen. CREATIVE
COMPUTING 9 (October 1983): 101-102.

Condo, Fred. SOFTSIDE (July 1983): 68, 70.

Sherouse, Vicki. BOOKLIST 80 (March 1, 1984):
1002.

Strehlo, Fred. PERSONAL SOFTWARE (January 1984):
92-93, 163.

Zapletal, Edward. COMPUTERS IN EDUCATION (April
1984): 28.

PROGRAM TITLE: THE BANK STREET WRITER

PUBLISHER: Scholastic, Inc.
           730 Broadway
           New York, NY 10003
           800-325-6149

SYSTEM REQUIREMENTS: Apple II+/48K/disk
drive/Applesoft BASIC

Apple IIe or IIc/64 or 128K/disk drive/Applesoft
BASIC

Commodore 64/64L/disk drive/BASIC

IBM PC or jr/64K/disk drive/BASIC

Printer

PACKAGE INCLUDES: 3 diskettes, documentation (96
pp.)

FUNCTIONS: This is an introductory word processing
program.

COMMENTS: This program has great appeal because it
is easy to use. The commands are relatively simple
to master in comparison to other word processing
programs. The manual is easy to comprehend and the
user can begin to approach mastery of the commands
in a very short time. One limitation is the amount
of memory available. As with some other original
word processing progams, there has been an
evolution of this software, and the reader is
cautioned to be aware of the date of publication
and make sure it is the latest version.

ADDITIONAL REVIEWS: Altman, Rick. PC WORLD 2
(November 1984): 234-236.

Chandler, H.W. JOURNAL OF LEARNING DISABILITIES 17
(January 1984): 55.

Bitter, Gary. INSTRUCTOR 93 (November/December
1983): 94-95.

DeKoven, Bernie, and Phil Wiswell. GIFTED CHILDREN
NEWSLETTER (November 1983): 17.

Furlong, M.S. SOCIAL EDUCATION 48 (April 1984):
300-301.

Korostoff, Marilyn. THE READING TEACHER 38 (October
1984): 94.

Miller, Philip. THE COMPUTING TEACHER 12 (December 1984/January 1985): 30-31.

Pagnoni, M. BYTE 9 (March 1984): 282-284.

Sherouse, Vicki. BOOKLIST 79 (November 1, 1983): 436.

Watt, M. POPULAR COMPUTING 2 (August 1983): 190-194.

PROGRAM TITLE: CROSSWORD MAGIC

PUBLISHER: L & S Computerware
           800-A Maude Avenue
           Mountain View, CA 94087
           (415) 962-8686

SYSTEM REQUIREMENTS: Apple II, II+, IIe/48K/disk drive/machine language

Atari 400 or 300/40K/disk drive/machine language

Printer optional

PACKAGE INCLUDES: 1 diskette, documentation (4 pp.)

FUNCTION: A program designed to produce crossword puzzles.

COMMENTS: An imaginative program that can used by the classroom teacher to create crossword puzzles for developing student vocabulary. The teacher can control the size of the puzzle and has the choice of producing hard copy or leaving the puzzle on disk. One drawback is that in creating the puzzle mistakes cannot be corrected once the entire word has been entered. One review involved using the program with 25 special education secondary school students. They found the opportunity to create their own puzzles interesting and worthwhile. This supports the fact that the program is easy to use and an enjoyable way to create social studies vocabulary reinforcement lessons.

ADDITIONAL REVIEWS: Bream, Elizabeth. EMERGENCY

LIBRARIAN 11 (May/June 1984): 35.

Dyrli, O.E. LEARNING 12 (February 1984): 28.

Hardiman, P.M.,and J.W. Hummel. JOURNAL OF LEARNING
DISABILITIES 17 (October 1984): 504-505.

PROGRAM TITLE: THE ELECTRONIC PENCIL

PUBLISHER: Blue Cat
          730 E. Katella Avenue
          Orange, CA 92667
          (714) 997-8244

SYSTEM REQUIREMENTS:IBM PC, AT, XT, or jr/128K/disk
drive/Machine language

TRS-80 1000, 1200 or 2000/128K/disk drive/ Machine
language

PACKAGE INCLUDES: 1 or 3 diskettes, documentation
(236 pp.)

FUNCTIONS: This is a general word processing
program that performs the usual functions of
editing, formating, and setting print
specifications.

COMMENTS: Overall, this is a very easy program to
master. The help screens are plentiful and serve
their purpose. The keyboard can be reprogramed if
you want to program in another language or desire a
different keyboard layout. An excellent
introductory program for teachers and students
because of its ease of use.

ADDTITIONAL REVIEWS: Green, Richard. INTERFACE AGE
8 (April 1983): 177-179.

Renne, Mark. INFOWORLD 6 (February 20, 1984): 50,
53-54.

Solomon, Gwen. ELECTRONIC LEARNING 4 (October
1984): 60.

Stapels, Betsy. CREATIVE COMPUTING 10 (March 1984):

126, 129-130, 134.

PROGRAM TITLE: HOMEWORD

PUBLISHER: Sierra On-Line, Inc.
          Sierra On-Line building
          Coarsegold, CA 93614
          (209) 683-6858

SYSTEM REQUIREMENTS: Apple II, II+, or IIe/64K/disk
drive/Assembly language

Commodore 64/64K/disk drive/Assembly language

IBM PCjr/128K/disk drive/Assembly language

Atari 800/64K/disk drive/Assembly language

Printer

PACKAGE INCLUDES:1 diskette, documentation (30
pp.), audio cassette

FUNCTIONS: This is a general word processing
program.

COMMENTS: A good choice for the nontypist and
anyone using a word processing program for the
first time because its command structure is
primarily visual while at the same time
intelligible and simple. This visual display of
commands is in the form of graphic icons rather
than command names. The basic functions of a word
processor can be learned within thirty minutes by
an intermediate-aged child. The tradeoff for this
simplicity is the fact that many high-powered
functions of a word processor, such as an 80-column
screen for displaying text, are not available.
Nonetheless, this program is ideally suited to the
beginner because of its documentation and unique
way of presenting commands.

ADDITIONAL REVIEWS: Anderson, Eric. BOOKLIST 81
(January 1, 1985): 661-662.

Carlson, Keith. BYTE 9 (October 1984): 271-275.

Edwards, John., Jr. (May 1984): 94-95.

Hetzel, Susan. POPULAR COMPUTING 3 (August 1984): 162-164.

Hunter, Bruce, and A.L. Wold. MEDIA AND METHODS 21 (September 1984): 3-31.

Kaplan, Howard. CLASSROOM COMPUTER LEARNING 4 (April/May 1984): 66-67.

Rasmussen, Alan. JOURNAL OF READING 28 (October 1984): 84-85.

Strehlo, Kevin. PERSONAL SOFTWARE (February 1984): 52, 53, 122.

PROGRAM TITLE: MAGIC SLATE

PUBLISHER: Sunburst Communications
          39 Washington Avenue
          Pleasantville, NY 10570
          (914) 769-5030

SYSTEM REQUIREMENTS: Apple II, II+, IIe, or IIc/128K/2 disk drives/printer/Applesoft BASIC

Graphics printer recommended

PACKAGE INCLUDES: 2 Diskettes (with 2 backups), documentation (203 pp. 62 pp.), 2 reference cards

FUNCTIONS: A general-use word processing program.

COMMENTS: One of the more popular word processing programs available because of its flexibility, excellent documentation, and variety of available functions. The program offers the user a 20-column, 40-column, and 80-column version from which to choose. The higher the text column available the more complex the functions and command structures. Thus the 20-column option of the program can be used by students as young as second grade while the 80-column option could be used by the teacher. The documentation is superior, providing the classroom teacher with many ideas that can easily be

incorporated into social studies lessons. The only
drawback is the difficulty in mastering printing
documents when using some of the program's more
sophisticated printing options such as typeface.

ADDITIONAL REVIEWS: Dana, Ann. TEACHING AND
COMPUTERS 2 (February 1985): 66.

Dana, Ann, and Barbara Sandy. ELECTRONIC LEARNING 4
(January 1985): 4.

Marks, Bonnie. CUE NEWSLETTER (January 1985): 23.

Olds, Henry F. CLASSROOM COMPUTER LEARNING 5 (March
1985): 22-25.

PROGRAM TITLE: MILLIKEN WORD PROCESSOR

PUBLISHER: Milliken Publishing Co.
            1100 Research Boulevard
            St. Louis, MO 63132
            (314) 991-4220

SYSTEM REQUIREMENTS: Apple II+, IIe, or
IIc/48K/disk drive/Applesoft Basic and Assembly
language

Color monitor and printer optional

PACKAGE INCLUDES: 1 master diskette (with backup),
1 storage diskette (unlimited backup),
documentation (35 pp.)

FUNCTIONS: This is a general-purpose word
processing program

COMMENTS: A user friendly word processing program,
the tutorial and documentation permit mastery
within a two- or three-hour period. As with other
easy-to-use word processing programs the more
sophisticated options, such as formatting, are not
available. The program is easy even for a young
student to learn because the screen display
consists of six lines which allows for large
letters, and the prompts appear above the text.

ADDITIONAL REVIEWS: Brady, Holly. CLASSROOM
COMPUTER LEARNING 5 (January 1985): 23-25.

Dana, Ann. TEACHING AND COMPUTERS 1 (October 1984):
65.

Solomon, Gwen. ELECTRONIC LEARNING 4 (October
1984): 61.

Steinberg, Ruth. CURRICULUM REVIEW 24
(January/February 1985): 45.

PROGRAM TITLE: THE NEWSROOM

PUBLISHER: Springboard Software, Inc.
           7807 Creekridge Circle
           Minneapolis, MN 55435
           (612) 944-3912

SYSTEM REQUIREMENTS: Apple II+, IIe, or IIc/64K

Commodore 64

IBM PC, PCjr/128K/DOS 2.1

Printer/ modem (optional)

PACKAGE INCLUDES: 2 diskettes, documentation (86
pp.)

FUNCTION: A graphics and word processing program.

COMMENTS: A way to help students develop a
classroom or school newspaper that can be used to
foster learning about current events. It is also a
useful career education tool for teaching about
journalism. The program is designed to permit the
user to create a banner, write text, and design a
layout. Photos can be included in the text, but
they must be drawn from the pool of over 600
graphics contained in the program. Newspaper
articles can be transmitted to other locations via
the wire service function of the program which
requires a modem. A fun and unique piece of
software.

PROGRAM TITLE: NEWSWORKS

PUBLISHER: Newsweek, Inc.
444 Madison Ave.
New York, NY 10022
(212) 350-4974

SYSTEM REQUIREMENTS: Apple IIe or IIc/64K/80 column
card

PACKAGE INCLUDES: 1 diskette (backups can be made
by user), documentation (40 pp.)

FUNCTION: This is a data diskette only. It must be
used with the spreadsheet function of the
AppleWorks integrated software package. This
program does not work without AppleWorks.

CONTENTS: An excellent way to introduce students to
the use of a data diskette for a spreadsheet. The
publisher has created three files including: world
community, U.S. economy, and U.S. government.
Information for each file is organized into at
least twenty different fields. For example, in the
world community file the data is categorized into
fields such as: income/capita,
people/doctor/literacy rate, etc. Twelve lesson
plans are provided giving the teacher and students
an excellent sampling of how NewsWorks could be
used. Also included in the documentation are
supplementary readings related to the data found in
the three files. This program represents an ideal
way for teachers to involve students in data
analysis without having to create a database.

PROGRAM TITLE: PFS:File
Report
Write
U.S. History
U.S. Government

PUBLISHER: Scholastic Software
730 Broadway
New York, NY 10003

SYSTEM REQUIREMENTS: Apple IIe or IIc/64K/2 disk

drives

IBM PC or jr/128K/disk drive

PACKAGE INCLUDES: Each program is accompanied by its own documentation (over 200 pp. each)

FUNCTION: Database management and word processing.

COMMENTS: An extensive review of each of these programs can be found in Chapter 5.

ADDITIONAL REVIEWS: Baraloto, A.R. ELECTRONIC LEARNING 5 (November/December 1985): 56-57.

White, C. S. SOCIAL EDUCATION 49 (January 1985): 59-62.

PROGRAM TITLE: THE PRINT SHOP

PUBLISHER: Broderbund Software
            17 Paul Drive
            San Rafael, CA 94903
            (415) 479-1170

SYSTEM REQUIREMENTS: Apple II+, IIe, IIc/48K/disk drive/printer

PACKAGE INCLUDES: 1 diskette (backup can be made), documentation (27 pp.)

FUNCTION: A graphics program.

COMMENTS: This program is popular and easy to use. It can design banners, greeting cards, stationery, and signs. Graphics can be chosen from this program or the supplemental graphic programs available from the publisher. The graphic editor permits the user to create an original graphic that can be saved onto a disk. A vareity of options for printing graphics and text are available. An excellent tool that can be used by very young students, and yet is enjoyable for adults also.

PROGRAM TITLE: SENSIBLE SPELLER   IV

PUBLISHER: Sensible Software, Inc.
          210 South Woodward, Suite 229
          Birminghan, MI 48011
          (313) 258-5566

SYSTEM REQUIREMENTS: Apple II, II+, IIe, or
IIc/48K/2 disk drives/Assembly language

PACKAGE INCLUDES: 1 program diskette (with backup),
2 dictionary diskettes (unlimited user made
backups), documentation (81 pp.)

FUNCTIONS: A program to be used with a wide variety
of compatible word processing programs for correct
spelling.

COMMENTS: Based on the RANDOM HOUSE DICTIONARY this
program is easy to use and of great value to anyone
working with a compatible word processing program.
Its design is excellent and the user will find it a
boon to proofreading for spelling errors. Words can
be added to and deleted from the dictionary base.
It has been given exceptionally favorable comments
by reviewers.

ADDITIONAL REVIEWS: Bitler, Tim. NIBBLE (April
1984): 65-69.

Mullins, C.J., and N.C. Mullins. SOFTWARE
SUPERMARKET (April 1984): 18-23.

Skapura, Bob. BOOKLIST 80 (January 1, 1984): 692.

PROGRAM TITLE: SOCIAL STUDIES FACTS FINDER (in
press)

PUBLISHER: HRM Software
          175 Tompkins Avenue
          Pleasantville, NY 10570
          (914) 769-6900

SYSTEM REQUIREMENTS: Apple IIe/64K/ProDOS or DOS
3.3/PFS:File

PACKAGE INCLUDES: 1 data diskette (must be used with PFS:File), teacher's guide (in press), junior and senior high school versions of activity cards for student use (in press)

FUNCTIONS: A database diskette and learning activities to be use with PFS:File

COMMENTS: An ideal resource for teaching students a variety of social studies concepts and skills related to databases. Three databases will be available and they include: The "Starter and States Pact," "Working America," and "Explorers." In the Starter and States Pact there is a file for each state which includes more than seven screens, or pages, of information including data on: population, family, politics, economics, education, environment, and miscellany. The accompanying activity cards promote higher order thinking skills. An excellent example of databases with well-conceived teaching suggestions. One of the best packages on the market.

PROGRAM TITLE: SQUARE PAIRS

PUBLISHER: Scholastic, Inc.
           730 Broadway
           New York, NY 10003
           (212) 505-3000

SYSTEM REQUIREMENTS: Apple II, II+, or IIe/48K/disk drive/Applesoft BASIC

Atari 400 or 800/32K/cassette recorder/BASIC

Commodore 64/64K/disk drive/BASIC

TI 99/4a/16K/cassette recorder/BASIC

VIC-20/13K/cassette recorder/BASIC

PACKAGE INCLUDES: 1 diskette or 1 cassette, documentation (16 pp.)

FUNCTION: This is a teacher tool that can be used to create memory and concentration activities.

COMMENTS: This program is a matching game which
gives students the opportunity to practice memory
and concentration tasks. The players take turns
matching items hidden behind squares which can be
changed by the teacher to handle any number of
social studies facts. For example, a teacher may
wish to teach countries and their capitals. The
information can be stored on blank disks and the
screen adjusted for up to 24 squares or cells of
information. Thus, it can be used by teachers of
primary school-aged children if a small number of
cells are used. Obviously, the learner is only
engaged in lower cognitive tasks such as the
knowledge level in Bloom's Taxonomy. It is,
however, fun to play and does promote learning.

ADDITIONAL REVIEWS: Baker, R.W. MICROCOMPUTING 8
(April 1984): 36.

Camuse, Ruth. SCHOOL SCIENCE AND MATHEMATICS 84
(February 1984): 164-166.

Hively, Wells. POPULAR COMPUTING (March 1984): 160.

Staples, Betsy. CREATIVE COMPUTING (April 1984):
62-63.

PROGRAM TITLE: SURVEY TAKER

PUBLISHER: Scholastic, Inc.
730 Broadway
New York, NY 10003
(800) 882-8222

SYSTEM REQUIREMENTS: Apple II+, IIe, or
IIc/48K/disk drive/BASIC

Printer and color monitor optional

PACKAGE INCLUDES: 1 diskette (with backup),
documentation (56 pp.)

FUNCTIONS: Information management.

COMMENTS: The user can create, edit, and print
surveys on any number of issues. Surveys can be

constructed using multiple choice, true/false, or
yes/no questions. Results can be printed in tables.
Instructions are generally clear and easy to
follow. Requires some supervision to ensure that
questions are well constructed and appropriate. An
excellent tool for both middle level and secondary
social studies teachers.

PROGRAM TITLE: TELOFACTS 1 AND 2

PUBLISHER: Dilithium Press
           921 Southwest Washington Street
           Pittock Building Suite 870
           Portland, OR 97210
           (503) 646-1842

SYSTEM REQUIRMENTS: Apple II, II+, IIe, or
IIc/64K/disk drive/C language

IBM PC or XT/128K/2 disk drives/color graphics
adapter card/C language

80-column card, 2nd disk drive

Printer and Mountain Computer card reader optional
for Apple

PACKAGE INCLUDES: Telofacts 1: 1 diskette,
Instructional manual (146 pp.)

Telofacts 2: 1 diskette, Instructional manual (136
pp.)

FUNCTIONS: Designs and performs statistical
analysis for surveys or questionnaire measurement
instruments.

COMMENTS: This program is an obvious boon to the
social studies teacher who needs survey research as
part of the curriculum. High school students could
use the program successfully. For younger students,
the teacher would have to operate the progam. It
is, however, flexible and easily mastered. The
manual and tutorial are helpful. It computes a
wide variety of statistical analyses. One very
peculiar aspect of the program is that it produces

a nice hardcopy of the results but not of the
survey once it is formatted by the program. In this
case, the teacher must make a typewritten copy of
what appears on the screen.

ADDITIONAL REVIEWS: Anderson, Eric. BOOKLIST 80
(July 1984): 1563.

Anderson, Eric. BOOKLIST 81 (January 1985):
661-662.

Cicciarella, C.F. COLLEGIATE MICROCOMPUTER 2
(Autumn 1984): 265-266.

Pettijohn, T.F. SOFTWARE SUPERMARKET (April 1984):
67.

Strehlo, Kevin. PERSONAL SOFTWARE (December 1983):
66-67.

PROGRAM TITLE: TEST AID

PUBLISHER: Infotools
           111 Country Club Lane
           Oxford, OH 45056
           (513) 523-8473

SYSTEM REQUIREMENTS: TRS-80 Color computer/32K/
disc drive or cassette recorder/BASIC/printer

PACKAGE INCLUDES: 1 diskette or 1 cassette (user is
permitted to make unlimited number of copies for
own use), documentation (17 pp.)

FUNCTIONS: This is a test-generating program that
can be used to create a bank of multiple-choice
test items.

COMMENTS: A database program that has been tailored
to perform the specific task of generating
multiple-choice items of up to 700 characters in
length. It is ideal for social studies teachers who
administer tests using this type of item. Questions
can be rearranged to create different forms of the
same exam. One problem with the program is the lack
of centering ability for the heading command. This

minor fault is the only one in what is otherwise a
very useful program.

ADDITIONAL REVIEWS: Garozzo, Michael. COLOR
COMPUTER (July 1984): 103-104.

Kueppers, Carol. THE RAINBOW (May 1984): 258-259.

PROGRAM TITLE: THINKTANK

PUBLISHER: Living Vidoetext, Inc.
          2432 Charleston Road
          Mountain View, CA 94043
          (415) 964-6300

SYSTEM REQUIREMENTS: Apple II, II+, IIe, or
III/64K/2 disk drives/PASCAL

IBM PC/256K/DOS 2.0/2 disk driveS/PASCAL

MacIntosh/128K/2 disk drives/PASCAL

Printer recommended

PACKAGE INCLUDES: Apple: 2 diskettes (user makes
backup), documentation (228 pp.)

IBM: 1 diskette (with one backup), documentation
(53 pp.)

FUNCTIONS: An information management program that
can serve as an outline organizer. Additionally,
the program can be employed as a word processor.

COMMENTS: This program is ideally suited to the
task of developing and organizing an outline. It
involves text entry and editing, and thus it can
also be used as a word processor. Most social
studies teachers, however, would find the program
very easy to use when applied to its primary
purpose, idea processing. The documentation is
instructive because of its clarity and
thoroughness. The novice user can become functional
with the program within minutes of sitting down and
using it. A relatively good example of the power of
a microcomputer, it is still a tool and thus its
value increases given the skill and ability of the

user.

ADDITIONAL REVIEWS: Baxter, Ernest. PERSONAL SOFTWARE (June 1984): 53.

Bonner, Paul. PERSONAL COMPUTING 8 (January 1984): 77, 79.

Carter, Richard. CLASSROOM COMPUTER LEARNING 4 (January 1984): 23.

Green, Doug, and Denise Green. INFOWORLD REPORT CARD (December 1, 1983): 37-38.

Heck, Mick. INTERFACE AGE 14 (October 1984): 87-89.

Hershey, W.R. BYTE 9 (May 1984): 189-90, 192, 194.

Owens, Peter. POPULAR COMPUTING 3 (April 1984): 187-189.

Schlobin, Roger C. LIFELINES/THE SOFTWARE MAGAZINE (September 1984): 18.

PROGRAM TITLE: VOLKSWRITER DELUXE

PUBLISHER: Lifetree Software, Inc.
           411 Pacific Street Suite 315
           Monterey, CA 93940
           (408) 373-4718

SYSTEM REQUIREMENTS: IBM PC/128K/2 disk drives/printer/PASCAL

PACKAGE INCLUDES: 1 diskette (user can make backup copy), documentation (150 pp.)

FUNCTIONS: A general word processing program.

COMMENTS: An easy and flexible program to use, this is a highly rated word processing program. Of note are the excellent editing, strong formatting, comprehensible documentation and tutorials, and concise on-line help. A good tool for secondary school teachers who either want to use it with students or for their own professional purposes.

ADDITIONAL REVIEWS: Lehrman, S.R. BYTE 9 (October 1984): 263-267.

Lombardi, John. INFOWORLD 6 (April 16, 1984): 42-43.

Pearlman, Dara. PC MAGAZINE (June 12, 1984): 195-201.

PROGRAM TITLE: WORD JUGGLER

PUBLISHER: Quark Incorporated
2525 West Evans
Denver, CO 80219
(800) 543-7711

SYSTEM REQUIREMENTS: Apple IIe or IIc/64K/disk drive/printer/Assembly language

Apple III/128K/disk drive/printer/Assembly language

PACKAGE INCLUDES: 1 diskette (with backup), documentation (112 pp.), keyboard template

FUNCTIONS: This is a general word processing program.

COMMENTS: The program is popular because it is easy to master and quite powerful. The well-written documentation is accompanied by a keyboard template that makes mastering commands simple. The user can learn the program within two hours. The editing function allows you to see the document exactly as it is printed. Menus are easy to bring up. The program has an interface that makes it compatible with PFS:File. Overall, a very highly rated word processing program.

ADDITIONAL REVIEWS: Ford, Doug. CREATIVE COMPUTING 9 (June 1983): 43-47.

Rubin, Charles. PERSONAL COMPUTING 3 (January 1984): 213-214.

CHAPTER 7

THE COMPUTER AND SOCIAL

EDUCATION ISSUES

A responsibility that is inherent in social studies education is the need to prepare students to become good citizens of their country and the world. The curriculum and instruction offered by social studies educators to meet this responsibility are referred to as social education. Given the overwhelming evidence that a revolution is indeed under way, it is apparent the role of the computer and its use should be a topic included in social education.

This final chapter raises some issues that social studies teachers might address in deciding how to include the topic of computers in the social education curriculum. Specifically, three areas will be dealt with in the chapter. First, the field of artificial intellingence will be examined. Included in this section will be ways to explore and promote human intelligence. This emerging paradigm of the human mind and new educative ways is called consciousness education. The development of a state of consciousness for computing is one way to describe the work of researchers in artificial intelligence. Second, the role of ethical behavior and moral development in relation to the computer and society is described. Finally, the chapter concludes with a futuristic perspective on the computer and lifestyles in the next century.

SOCIAL STUDIES AND EMERGING PARADIGMS: ARTIFICIAL INTELLINGENCE AND CONSCIOUSNESS EDUCATION

Are machines capable of thinking like people? How is the thinking of a computer similar to and different from human thinking? What exactly is thinking? These are psychological, and perhaps anthropological, questions that social studies teachers must raise. Failure to address these questions would result in inadequately developing student understanding of individual's and humanity's relationship to technology. And, this could have dire cultural consequences when the next generation comes of age in the twenty-first century (Turkel, 1984).

This section will attempt to answer these questions, first by chronicling the accomplishments and stumbling blocks of computer scientists and other researchers in the field of artificial intelligence. This will serve as a background for answering the second and third questions which involve a description of the theory and research of consciousness education, an emerging paradigm about human thinking that is already showing educative potential for social studies education. A role and justification for including consciousness education and artificial intelligence in the social studies curriculum will serve as a conclusion to this section.

Can the computer really emulate human thought? To some this very idea seems illogical. Others point out theological and philosophical questions that mechanical thought raises, such as what is the nature of human thought if machines can be programmed to think (Searle, 1980; Turkle, 1984)? In a brilliant analogy Seymour Papert, the father of LOGO, provides a tongue-in-cheek description of how human beings did not solely rely on researching birds in their efforts to create a means for human flight (Papert, 1980). Rather, they studied a wide range of phenomena and used diverse methodologies in arriving at a principle, Bernoulli's Law, that accounts for how both birds and machines are capable of flight. Papert's point is that the same convergence of a variety of disciplines is true for those doing research in the development of artificial intelligence. Similarly, just as our concept of flight has been adjusted to accommodate the phenomenon of human flight, our definition of thought is being modified in relation to developments in artificial intelligence and consciousness education.

Computer engineering, cognitive psychology, and linguistics are representative of the diverse fields that have come together as scientists endeavor to refine artificial intelligence. These research efforts fall into two categories, basic and applied. So far, the nature of artificial intelligence, as seen through the work of applied

research, is much more limited and only a rough
approximation of human intelligence. Applications
orientated research into artificial intelligence
has resulted in what computer users refer to as
expert systems. Examples of expert systems are a
game of chess played by a computer which
consistently beats a skilled player or the
diagnosis a doctor obtains via a computer. Seymour
Papert's educational program, LOGO, is another
example of artificial intelligence as an expert
system.

Expert systems can help define the work of
applied artificial intelligence if one thinks of an
expert system as focusing on a highly specific area
of knowledge and then analyzing information using
certain rules of thumb which follow an IF/THEN
format, a crude form of intelligence. Because of
IF/THEN statements the machine is able to
rationalize some decision. There are those who
would argue that this does not represent thought at
all and to conceive of expert systems as
intelligence presents serious philosophical
questions about the nature of human beings and what
constitutes thought (Turkle, 1984).

To help resolve this argument of what
constitutes thought and intelligence, the British
mathematician and pioneer, Alan Turing, in an
effort to develop electronic digital computers,
proposed an investigation commonly called the
Turing test. Essentially, the test consists of a
room in which there is a computer terminal that
could be hooked up to one of two sources: a human
being or a computer. The object of the test is for
the user to determine through interactions with the
terminal whether the computer or the human is
actually responding. If the user cannot tell
whether it is the computer or the human, then,
Turing claims, the computer is thinking and should
be considered intelligent.

Although a clever argument it is a moot one
since a machine capable of actually passing the
Turing test does not yet exist. The construction of
such a computer poses is as yet an insurmountable
hurtle to researchers of artificial intelligence.
The expert systems that do exist cannot process
language in a natural way. Thus, expert systems can
easily be identified by the user applying the
Turing test if the user supplies irrelevant

responses or vocabulary not contained in the
program. In other words, expert systems only seem
smart if the user confines interlocutions to
remarks the program can recognize. The development
of a program that uses natural language processing
remains one of the central hurdles faced by
researchers. How does one create a computer program
to understand all the complexities, subtleties, and
ambiguities of human language systems? An even more
basic problem is how to create a machine that can
operate with the speed and range of a human mind ?

The continuation of basic research into
artificial intelligence not only faces the problems
of natural language processing but also of
replicating the amounts of knowledge and multiple
ways of processing information the human mind has
at its disposal. Neuroscientists who study how the
brain functions are revising their theories about
how the brain actually works. Traditionally, the
human brain was seen as a vast switching network
consisting of billions of individual neurons that
communicated with one another through electric
impulses. This view has been revised and now the
belief is that neurons actually work in large
cooperative groups and these interact with complex
electromagnetic fields that pervade the brain
(Lerner, 1984). An additional illustration of the
influence of diverse fields upon one another, is
that artificial intelligence researchers hope that
theoretical revisions in brain research will guide
their own efforts to create computers that can
think like humans and one day pass the Turing test.

According to the revised model of brain
functioning described by Lerner, called the
cooperative action model, thoughts and perceptions
are encoded in the changing patterns of the
electromagnetic fields rather than the impulses of
individual neurons (1984). As the large group of
neurons act in cooperation to generate the
electromagnetic fields these fields reflect back
onto the neurons and influence their activity. This
action might be described as being holistic and
synergistic in the nature of its effects.

The study of the brain cell's collective
electromagnetic activity has been made possible
through computer based techniques of research. As
computer based research techniques into the
cooperative action of the brain's neural and

electromagnetic functioning continues it is
apparent that building a computer that functions in
the same way as the human brain would be quite
different from any computer that has been developed
thus far. For example, all computers, whether
serial or parallel, operate by sending discrete
signals. Albeit, this is with amazing speed but it
fails to approach the magnitude of the brain's
capacity and speed. In fact, for a computer to
replicate the brain's activity it would have to
operate on a continuous signal. Similarly, the
communication among the computer's various elements
would be via electromagnetic waves spreading
continuously through the computing elements rather
than by signals traveling along separate
communication lines linking the individual
elements. It is for these reasons that a computer
capable of passing the Turing test, or otherwise
replicating human states of consciousness, does not
exist and probably never will.

As artificial intelligence researchers
continue to work at what are so far insurmountable
problems of creating a computer capable of
consciousness, educational psychologists are
redefining what constitutes human consciousness
itself. A state of consciousness has been defined
by Tart (1975) as a pattern, an overall style of
psychological functioning at any one time. States
of consciousness research is an area of psychology
that is rapidly gaining respectability and
professional attention (Grof, 1985). A theoretical
structure of states of consciousness, its
relationship to education, and examples of methods
have been described by Roberts (1985). Educational
internventions to promote the development of the
resident abilities in a variety of states
constitute what Roberts calls consciousness
education.

Many consciousness education methods emphasize
relaxation training and facilitating the use of
both hemispheres of the brain. Examples of
consciousness education techniques that are
frequently found in social studies education
include cognitive guided imagery (DeVoe and Render,
1982) and memory techniques (Ostrander and
Ostrander, 1982). Similarly, the direct teaching of
intuition in social studies has been advocated
(Shores, 1984). Inquiry into thanatology, the study

of the human experience of death, and the
exploration of dreams would be appropriate themes
for social studies teachers to consider in relation
to consciousness education. Biofeedback, the
ability of the mind to enter an altered state of
consciousness and direct bodily functions such as
skin temperature, is an area of psychology and
physical health, that should be addressed in
consciousness education curriculum for social
studies.

I would urge elementary and secondary social
studies teachers to address consciousness education
from both perspectives, artificial and multiple
states of human consciousness, for the following
reasons: First, nativistic research with elementary
school-aged children suggests they perceive
computers from a perspective of animism. Piaget
(1960) described animism as ascribing to inanimate
objects abilities such as movement or thinking.
Examples of this would be the explanation of a
young child that clouds "go away" or "the computer
is smarter at a game." The young child needs to
begin working at a conceptual definition of what
thinking is. How is human thinking different from a
computer's way of "thinking"? "What are feelings?"
and "Do computers have them?" are examples of
animistic questions that an elementary school-aged
child might raise. Elementary social studies
teachers should address these kinds of queries.
Consciousness education can help a child apprehend
the multitudinous dimensions of human
consciousness. At the same time, distinctions
between the human mind and artificial intelligence
can and should be drawn. Not to do so invites the
possibility that future generations will become
overdependent on the computer in place of human
contact and suffer a further erosion in our ability
to meet our primary human need of forming intimate
social relationships (Turkel, 1984).

Another important consideration in the
rationale for incorporating consciousness education
is the innate need for humans to alter
consciousness (Weil, 1971). Unfortunately, far too
many students learn to meet this need by abusing
such substances as tobacco, alcohol, and other
psychoactive plants and chemicals. Throughout the
childhood and adolescent stages of development
students should be finding natural and healthy ways

to alter consciousness. Ideal places for infusing natural and healthy ways of altering consciousness, and examining the human need to do so, into the curriculum are traditional social studies disciplines including: psychology, which is a direct study of human consciousness; geography, which examines states of consciousness related phenomena such as orientation to space and time; and anthropology, the social studies discipline that appropriately examines how cultural groups such as the Yanamomo Indians of South America ritualistically alter consciousness. Braun (1981) and Haney (1979) have described the role of consciousness education as it relates to global studies. Thus, there is strong justification for studying states of consciousness in social studies, as there is for studying it in other curricular areas like mathematics (Noddings and Shore, 1984), language arts (Hayes, 1975), and the fine arts (Edwards, 1979).

A review of the preceding reveals tentative answers to the questions posed at the beginning of this section. Machines do not seem capable of thinking like people. A computing system has not yet passed the Turing test because the development of artificial intelligence has thus far been limited to expert systems. While expert systems process a great deal of information with incredible speed and ease, they do not have the range or variety of mental processes available to humans, such as the abilities to deal with natural language or spontaneously produce imagery. Human thought has been defined as the ability to access any number of mental patterns of functioning and use the abilities that are resident in that pattern--which raises a final question. If scientists are right and we are only using a small percentage of our brain's capacity, how might consciousness education, and the use of computers, help us tap into this vast reserve of potential?

Ethics is a second theme that should be addressed as part of the social education curriculum for the next generation of Americans. The civic, social, and moral issues must be identified and faced as the Infomation Age develops.

COMPUTERS AND MORAL DEVELOPMENT

In an open letter to social studies teachers,
David Matthews, the former Secretary of Health,
Education, and Welfare, urged that civic competency
and social responsibility be infused in social
studies curriculum at all levels (Matthews, 1985).
Implied in his discussion is that the development
of civic competence and social responsibility must
include consideration of the appropriate use of
technology, such as the computer, in our culture.
The computer and its relationship to civic
competence and social responsibility can be seen in
two ways. First, the use of computers and their
role in society can be examined as a values issue.
For example, what are just uses of a computer in
society to collect information about its citizenry
and what human rights abuses, such as violation of
privacy, does a computer portend for the
twenty-first century? Second, the computer can be a
vehicle for promoting social and moral development
when used as a learning tool as part of values or
civic education programs. This section will
describe the computer from both perspectives, as a
value issue worthy of examination itself and as a
learing tool for promoting development of
democratic and humanistic values.

Social studies educators, among others, have
begun the critical task of raising fundamental
ethical and moral questions in relation to
computers and the future direction of our society
(Johnson, 1984; Kreidler, 1984; Marx, 1985; Glenn
and Klassen, 1983; Hepburn, 1983; Riedesel and
Clements, 1985; Turkel, 1985). A summary list of
the questions and issues raised would include the
following:

1) Will the increased dependency on
computers concentrate power in the hands
of a bureaucracy that becomes more
autocratic as power increases ? Will
large data banks give the government or
other agencies in the private sector more
control over the political and social
behavior of its citizens?

2) How will increased use of computers
affect interpersonal relations? Will we

see an overall decrease in face-to-face
human interaction and an increase in
feelings of alienation?

3) What effects on career satisfaction
will occur as a result of increased
computerization and robotics in the
workplace? Can the computer take the
drudgery out of menial tasks without
leaving millions jobless?

4) As people come to trust computerized
banking and financial transactions, will
electronic theft become an unsolvable
problem?

5) How is an author's right to copyright
work affected in an Information Age? What
is a fair profit for a
software/electronics author?

6) Will the access to computer technology
and potential for improving our lives be
limited to the upper classes in the
society? How can a democratic society
promote equal technological access?

7) What are the responsibilities and
obligations of computer manufacturers and
vendors in a "free" enterprise economy?
As new models of hardware and software
flood the market, does CAVEAT EMPTOR
apply to software that is sold to
unsuspecting consumers who will find it
incompatible with their computing system?

These and other social, political, and moral
questions should be addressed by social studies
educators in preparing students to become members
of society. There are three distinct approaches to
values education which can help students begin to
address these questions. The use of moral dilemmas
as a process for promoting moral growth has been
utilized with students at all levels (Kohlberg,
1983). With training, hypothetical dilemmas can be
developed by teachers which focus on any number of
moral issues related to the computer. A dilemma is
created when competing moral claims such as

A value issue of computers is whether students from all segments of our society will have equal access to computer technology. (Photo courtesy of the Museum of Science and Industry, Chicago, Illinois)

property and law come into conflict. For example, a
real life dilemma that many students face involves
copyright and the illegal reproduction of software.
Is it ever all right to illegally reproduce
software? What should an individual do if a friend
provides pirated software that helps classmates
complete school assignments? In this situation two
competing moral claims, law and affiliation, are
brought into conflict. Does the end, helping
students be more successful in academic work,
justify the means of distributing pirated software?
A considerable body of research indicates that the
use of moral dilemmas is an excellent way to help
students reason in more sophisticated ways (Leming,
1985).

    Similarly, values clarification strategies can
incorporate issues related to computers and society
(Simon, 1978). Unlike moral dilemmas which consist
of classroom discussion led by the teacher to
explore moral reasoning, values clarification
consists of numerous activities designed to help
students express and appreciate value positions.
Rank ordering a list of value positions or polling
the class about a value position are examples of
values clarification activities. As with moral
dilemmas, values clarification activities can be
developed by the teacher to promote consideration
of issues related to computers and their ethical
use. An excellent example of a computerized values
clarification simulation that involves students in
resolving current and historically based ethical
issues is DECISIONS, DECISIONS (See Chapter 4 for a
review). In this series teams of players are given
roles to assume and put into confrontational
situations. The objective is to work to resolve the
nature of the conflict while working through
conflicting values of members of the group.

    A third approach to values education that can
incorporate computer issues is values analysis
(Banks, 1973). The process of values analysis
involves the student in identifying an issue or
describing the problem; identifying alternative
solutions to the problem; hypothesizing and/or
collecting data on the likely consequences for each
alternative; arriving at a decision; and justifying
the decision (See figure 7.1). Values analysis
might examine questions such as do minority,
disadvantaged, or women students enroll in computer

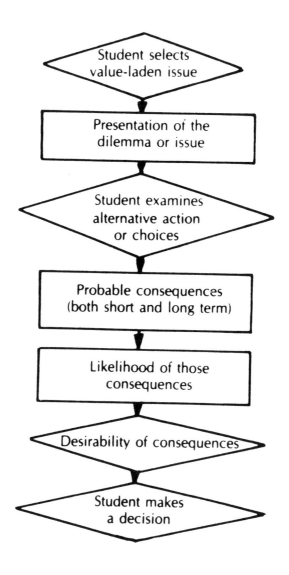

Figure 7-1

A flowchart representation of the of the values analysis process.

science courses as frequently as white males?

In addition to considering the computer's being an issue in itself, the computer can be of assistance as part of the values analysis or clarification process (Braun and Slobodzian, 1981). Since both these approaches involve the collection and analysis of data, the computer is an ideal tool for these tasks. Databases and spreadsheets are types of software that could help students collect and categorize data collected on any value issue being studied. An excellent example of a preexisting database that could be used by social studies teachers who wish to take up a values analysis is NewsWorks. Students could use this database to examine the educational levels obtained by women in the Third World versus Western society (see Chapter 5 for a more detailed discussion of NewWorks).

The University of Michigan has developed an exciting interactive communications simulation titled "Arab-Israeli Exercise." This is an excellent way for social studies students to explore values from an international-political perspective as the participants take on the roles of various leaders in the Mideast and then must interact with each other via telecommunications linked to the mainframe computer on the Ann Arbor campus. Social studies educators interested in learing more about this simulation can call the director of Interactive Communications Simulations at the School of Education, University of Michigan, at (313) 763-6716.

As the quality of software improves in its ability to promote the learning of social studies skills and knowledge, there may be an increased emphasis on the role of the teacher to help students acquire values, develop character, and interpersonal skills (Leonard, 1984). Any one of the three approaches to values education described above can be applied to the process of helping students arrive at ethical principles that should guide their relationship to computers. It is critical in preparing students for life in the twenty-first century that social studies instruction raise social, political, and moral questions that center on the computer and its use in our culture. Failure to address the issue of computers and information technology as part of

values education will leave a serious gap in the
social studies teachers' mission of developing
civic competence and social responsibility in
themselves and their students.

COMPUTERS AND LIFESTYLES: A FUTURISTIC PERSPECTIVE

The inventors of technological wonders such as
the automobile, indoor plumbing, the airplane, and
television certainly did not foresee the enormous
impact these inventions would have on our culture.
Similarly, those individuals who have sparked the
computer revolution, before Jobs and Wozniak burst
on the scene, did not conceive how rapidly the
computer would invade the workplace and affect the
ways millions of people throughout the world
conduct human activity. In the remarkably short
period of forty years the computer has been reduced
from a gigantic, expensive, and enormously complex
mass of wires and tubes that only a select group of
specialists could operate to a compact unit that
fits inside a briefcase.

The historical trend of miniaturization and
reliance on the capacity of the computer to process
information and perform a variety of tasks will
continue to accelerate. In his brilliant look at
the accelerating rate of change and its potentially
deleterious effects, Toeffler (1970) warned us to
be prepared for change or suffer from a malaise he
calls "future shock." Since it is the social
studies teacher's responsibility to provide social
education, helping students to anticipate change
should be part of the social studies curriculum.
The purpose of this concluding section is to
familiarize the social studies teachers with some
of the changes futurists speculate may occur as a
result of advances in the computerization of
society. The following discussion will also serve
as a chapter review since many of the predictions
and observations rendered by futurists include
elements of the previous themes.

Included in a broad list of internal factors
shaping the careers of the future are brain/mind
capabilities and values. The relationship between
these factors and the computer are evident in the
three scenarios for occupations in the year 2000
that Borchard envisions (see Figure 7.2).

Three Scenarios for Occupations in the Year 2000

PERSONALITY TYPE	1·LITTLE CHANGE	2·EXTERNAL TRANSFORMATION	3·INTERNAL TRANSFORMATION
Realistic *Technically & Athletically Inclined People*	Electronic Technician, Robot Technician, Pre-Fab Construction Worker, Cable-TV Technician, Medical Technician	Laser Technician, Solar Technician, Space Station Technician, Satellite Communication, Bionic Limb Technician	Brain/Mind Lab Technician, Bioenergetic Technician, Actualization Abode Carpenter, Thought Transmission and Recording Technician, Health Food Farmer
Investigative *Abstract Problem Solvers*	Pollution Control Scientist, Systems Analyst, Nuclear Engineer, Computer Scientist, Intelligence Analyst	Space Medicine Scientist, Computer Scientist Medical Analyst, Space Habitation Analyst, Extraterrestrial Geologist, Weapons Disposal Engineer	Genetic Engineer, Well-Being Medical Doctor, Mind Expansion Researcher, Human Communications Specialist, Peace Scientist
Artistic *Idea Creators*	Graphics Design Commercial Artist, Cable-TV Writer, Conservation Architect, Military Musician, Curriculum Developer	Computer-Assisted Design and Computer Graphics Artist, International Satellite Communications Script Writer, Solar Energy Architect, Computer Musician, Right Brain Curriculum Developer	Thought Transmission Artist, Human Expansion Writer, Human Milieu Architect, Mind Expansion Musician, Whole Brain Curriculum Developer
Social *People Helpers*	Nurse, Stress Psychologist, Marriage/Divorce Counselor, Public Education Teacher, Geriatrics Nurse	Computerized Medicine Nurse, Space Psychologist, New Modes of Living Counselor, Private Computer Learning Facilitator, Retirement Longevity Counselor	Psychic Healer, Actualization Psychologist, Mind/Body/Spirit Counselor, Personal Enlightenment Tutor, Age 70 + Career Counselor
Enterprising *People Influencers*	Industrial Robot Salesperson, Hospital Administrator, Military Officer, Electronics Office Manager, Criminal Lawyer	Solar Car Salesperson, Electronics Medical Diagnosis Center Manager, International Peace Project Officer, International Data Bank Manager, Euthanasia Lawyer	Rapid Learning Machine Salesperson, Actualization Center Manager, Quality of Life Projects Manager, Brain/Mind Data Bank Manager, Genetic Manipulation Lawyer
Conventional *Data & Detail People*	Data Entry Clerk, Word Processing Specialist, Medical Records Technician, Computer Programmer, Accountant	International Data Base Clerk, Paperless Office Administrative Aide, Electronics Medical Diagnostic Records Technician, Computer Security Inspector, Computer Accountant	Brain/Mind Data Bank Clerk, Thought Transmission Recorder, Actualization Center Administrative Assistant, Psychic Research Aide, Personal Efficiency Advisor

This chart shows what job titles might be found in Holland's Occupational Environment hexagon (see Figure 2) in three different scenarios of the year 2000.

Reprinted with permission from THE FUTURIST, published by the World Future Society, 4916 St. Elmo Ave., Bethesda, Maryland, 20814.

Figure 7-2

The Work Force: Key Characteristics

Pre-WWII	"TV Babies"	"Computer Babies"
Preferred Work Environment		
Power hierarchy: work your way up the ladder of success.	Quality circles and teams; participatory management.	Autonomy; individual works alone, least amount of supervision.
Goal		
Get the job done because it is good for the company, good for the nation.	Get meaningful experience from doing the job; personal growth.	Get job done so individual can use his own leisure time more satisfactorily.
Work Medium		
Assembly line; human labor.	Mainframe computers.	Personal (desk-top) computers.
Time Values		
9-to-5; overtime.	9-to-5; flexitime begins.	Flexitime, flexiplace.
Information and Enculturation Media		
Radio in the living room; newsreels at movie theater.	Television news; rock-n-roll; transistor radios.	Walkman; VCRs; music videos.
Consumption		
Brand-name buying; few choices available, few demanded.	More choices available.	More choices demanded.

Reprinted with permission from THE FUTURIST, published by the World Future Society, 4916 St. Elmo Ave., Bethesda, Maryland, 20814.

Figure 7-3

As for more specific predictions, the workforce of the future may conduct much of their work from their homes (Toeffler, 1980; Eder, 1983). In addition to increased productivity, possible benefits of a home based workforce include a significant savings in energy and automobile usage. Of course, this may be accompanied by such social changes as disruption of traditional family roles and increased feelings of isolation. In describing the key characteristics of the workforce from the past three generations, Deutsch has described specific values that distinguish these succeeding groups (see Figure 7.3).

Futurists look at current trends in developing their scenarios for the future. In regard to a specific career, such as medicine, significant impact can already be seen as a result of artificial intelligence and serious ethical questions that must be faced because of computer related technology. Software is available to physicians that converts patients' symptoms into if/then statements, a form of an expert system, which assists the physician in diagnosing the illness and selecting a form of therapy. Computers play a vital role in prolonging human life and shaping values. For example, consider the moral reasoning involved when the agonizing decision is made to allow the life of a brain-dead patient to expire naturally. Euphemistically, this is known as "pulling the plug," a harsh and slangy way of describing euthanasia or "mercy killing." Computers also aid a great number of disabled people. This includes the deaf, blind, and even those with paralysis of limbs (McWilliams, 1984). Obviously, the computer's word processing and information processing capabilities have revolutionized office practices of the medical profession.

Based on their current studies, futurists tell us sweeping changes will take place in almost all careers within the next twenty years as a result of computerization. In addition to the workplace we can expect to see our homes and schools affected by computers. Perhaps in the not too distant future many children, and adult learners, will use a computer at home to master the curriculum (Mason, 1984). Videodiscs, interactive video, and computerized telecommunication will transform the activities of the teacher. Students may only attend school for social and interpersonal development. The teacher in the future will be viewed by students as a resource person who helps them choose from an incredible array of learning technology, most of it computer based or assisted. Thus, the teacher and students would only meet face to face for experiences designed to foster value and interpersonal development. It is imperative that teachers and society prepare to deal with the resulting sense of isolation that futurists warn computers may unleash.

In addition to education being directly brought into the home as a result of computers, many other home based activities will be affected by computers. Already microchips can help start coffee brewing in the morning or relay a message to the police department if a burglar detection system is tripped. The operation of the car in the future might be through a computerized guidance system. All the driver would have to do is place a piece of software into the computer and the route and traffic conditions will be monitored by the machine. It is unlikely, however, that the driver will be headed for work.

The best we can do is speculate and make educated guesses about the future as a result of the transformation of Western society by an Information Age. One thing that is clear, however, is the need for social studies teachers to prepare their students for entrance into that society. The purpose of this chapter has been to point out some areas for the social education curriculum that will be influenced by computerization. It is more than likely that future generations will develop unique ways of learning and establishing values as a result of the computer. Additionally, we can foresee that social studies education will be as essential as it ever has been.

BIBLIOGRAPHY

Abelson, Hal. LOGO FOR THE APPLE II. New York: McGraw-Hill, 1982.

Allen, John; Michael Burke; and John Johnson.
THINKING ABOUT (TLC) LOGO. New York: Holt, Rinehart
and Winston, 1983.

American Psychological Association. STATES OF
CONSCIOUSNESS. New York: Teachers College Press,
1981.

A comprehensive instructional unit that can be used
with secondary school students to introduce the
topic of states of consciousness. Included is a
workbook with a variety of useful learning
activities. The emphasis is on having students make
observations and analyze the data they collect for
similarities and differences.

Balajthy, E. "Artificial Intelligence and the
Teaching of Reading and Writing by Computers."
JOURNAL OF READING (October 1985): 23-32.

Banks, J.A. TEACHING STRATEGIES FOR THE SOCIAL
STUDIES: INQUIRY VALUING AND DECISION-MAKING.
Reading, Mass: Addison-Wesley, 1973.

Borchard, D.C. "New Choices: Career Planning in a
Changing World." THE FUTURIST 18 (August 1984):
37-46.

Braun, J.A. "Consciousness Education and the Global
Perspective." THE SOCIAL STUDIES 74
(September/October 1983): 201-205.

Braun, J.A. , and K.A. Slobodzian. "Can Computers
Teach Values?" EDUCATIONAL LEADERSHIP 39 (April
1982): 508-512.

Cornish, Edward. THE COMPUTERIZED SOCIETY: LIVING
AND WORKING IN AN ELECTRONIC AGE. Bethesda, Md.:
World Future Society, 1985.

A collection of more than twenty articles from past
issues of THE FUTURIST that deal with a variety of
issues related to computers. Included are essays on
careers, universities, sex education, and
videotext. An excellent resource for the teacher.
With assistance, many articles could be
comprehended by secondary school social studies

students.

Deutsch, R.E. "Tomorrow's Work Force: New Values in the Workplace." THE FUTURIST 19 (December 1985): 8-11.

The changes in values and needs of "computer babies" are described. Fiercely independent, they will also probably sweep aside the more traditional values established by the previous generations. Leisure time will be highly valued as will the use of videodiscs and other media for information and enculturation.

Deutsch, R. E. "Tomorrow's Work Force: New Values in the Workplace." THE FUTURIST 19 (December 1985): 8-11.

DeVoe, M.W., and Gary F. Render. "Gestalt Strategies for Elementary Social Studies." SOCIAL EDUCATION 46 (May 1982): 348-352.

Dreyfus, H. WHAT COMPUTERS CAN'T DO: THE LIMITS OF ARTIFICIAL INTELLIGENCE. New York: Harper/Colophon, 1979.

Eder, P.F. "Telecommunications: The Stay-at-home Work Force of the Future." THE FUTURIST 17 (June 1983): 90-94.

Edwards, Betty. DRAWING ON THE RIGHT SIDE BRAIN. Los Angeles: J.P. Tarcher, 1979.

Estes, W.K. "Is Human Memory Obsolete?" AMERICAN SCIENTIST 68 (January-February 1980): 62-69.

A comparison of human and computer memories is made and the research suggests that there is little likelihood that one will replace the other. Part of this is based on their unique modes of operation. A long-term goal of research is to use a computer's memory to remedy failures in human memory, perhaps a "mental prosthetics" that takes over some functions of the human brain.

Feigenbaum, E.A. THE FIFTH GENERATION: ARTIFICIAL INTELLIGENCE AND JAPAN'S COMPUTER CHALLENGE TO THE WORLD. Reading, Mass.: Addison-Wesley, 1983.

The race between Japan and the United States to gain supremacy in the computer industry is described. This includes tactics being used by both nations as they try to develop knowledge information processing systems or super-expert systems. Several options available to American researchers and developers are outlined so they may outwit the Japanese. The authors favor a concentrated effort for nation

Foshay, A., and Irving Morrisset. BEYOND THE SCIENTIFIC: A COMPREHENSIVE VIEW OF CONSCIOUSNESS. Boulder, Colo.: Social Science Consortium, 1978.

Glenn, A.D., and D.L. Klassen "Computer Technology and the Social Studies." THE EDUCATIONAL FORUM (Winter 1983): 213-216.

Grof, Stanislov. "Modern Consciousness Research and Human Survival." REVISION 8 (Summer/Fall 1985): 27-40.

Hanvey, R.G. AN ATTAINABLE GLOBAL PERSPECTIVE. New York: Global Perspectives in Education, 1979.

Harvey, Brian. COMPUTER SCIENCE LOGO STYLE. Cambridge, Mass.: MIT Press, 1985.

Hepburn, M. "The New Information Technology: Critical Questions for Social Science Educators." In R.B. Ableson, ed. USING MICROCOMPUTER IN THE SOCIAL STUDIES CLASSROOM. Boulder, Colo.: ERIC Clearinghouse for Social Studies, 1983.

Hofstadler, D. GODEL, ESCHER, BACH: AN ETERNAL GOLDEN BRAID. New York: Basic Books, 1979.

Johnson, D.W. COMPUTER ETHICS: A GUIDE FOR THE NEW AGE. Elgin, Illinois: Brethern, 1984.

Knauer, G. "Computer Programs for the Mind: New Ways to Learn." THE FUTURIST 20 (March-April 1986): 33-35.

A speculative essay on how computer programs will mean new links between man and machine. Describes how computerized psychology is moving beyond the static input/output of the electronic spreadsheet and statistical data processing to a new, interactive partnership between integrated circuitry. Desribes the work of Robert Dilts who is applying neuro-linguistic programming principles, a "behavioral technology," to the creation of software to teach strategies for learning. Also describes the efforts of Timothy Leary to develop interactive psychological software.

Kohlberg, L., Charles Levine, and Alexander Hewer. MORAL STAGES: A CURRENT FORMULATION AND RESPONSE TO CRITICS. New York: S. Kraeger, 1983.

Kreidler, W.J. "Teaching Computer Ethics." ELECTRONIC LEARNING (January 1984): 54-57.

Krutch, J. EXPERIMENTS IN ARTIFICIAL INTELLIGENCE. Indianapolis: Howard W. Sans, 1981.

A good introduction to the topic. Included are some very low level examples of expert systems, including modification of the famous ELIZA or psychotherapist program, that can programmed into a home computer.

Leming, J.S. "Research on Social Studies Curriculum and Instruction: Interventions and Outcomes in the Socio-Moral Domain." In William B. Stanley, ed. REVIEW OF RESEARCH IN SOCIAL STUDIES EDUCATION: 1976-1983. Washington, D.C.: National Council for the Social Studies, 1985.

An indepth look at the field of values education intervention from three perspectives: values analysis, values clarification, and cognitive-moral development. Also considered are school practices designed to forster democratic principles and just communities. Recommendations for future research efforts in this aspect of social education conclude what is an excellent resource.

Leonard, George. "The Great School Reform Hoax."
ESQUIRE (April 1984): 47-56.

Lerner, E.J. "Why Can't a Computer Be More Like a
Brain." HIGH TECHNOLOGY (August 1984): 34-41.

Mason, R., L. Jennings, and Robert Evans. XANADU:
THE COMPUTERIZED HOME OF TOMMOROW AND HOW IT CAN BE
YOURS TODAY! Washington, D.C.: Acropolis Books
Ltd., 1983.

Matthews, David. "Civic Intelligence." THE SOCIAL
STUDIES 49 (November/December 1985): 678-681.

McGrath, Diane. "Artificial Intelligence: A
Tutorial for Educators." ELECTRONIC LEARNING
(September 1984): 39-43.

McWilliams, P.A. PERSONAL COMPUTERS AND THE
DISABLED. New York: Doubleday, 1984.

A witty and good elementary-level look at what
computers are and how they operate begins this
book. Topics from ROM to electronic mail are
covered. Only Chapters Four through Eight, out of a
total of twelve, directly address the disabled. The
remainder of the book covers such issues as
purchasing a computer and a brief treatment of
basic steps in programming. As a conclusion, the
author provides an annotated list of equipment,
with out-of-date prices, and a list of resources.
In its favor are the humorous captions under the
plentiful illustrations. The readability level of
this book would be at the instructional level for
most high school students.

Noddings, Nel, and Paul J. Shore. AWAKENING THE
INNER EYE: INTUITION IN EDUCATION. New York:
Teachers College Press, 1984.

Ostrander, S., and Lynn Schroder. SUPERLEARNING.
New York: Dell Publishing Company, 1979.

Papert, Seymour. MINDSTORMS: CHILDREN, COMPUTERS,
AND POWERFUL IDEAS. New York: Basic Books, 1980.

A monumental book that advocates the use of

computers with children in much different ways than
is typically encountered in school. Rather than the
computer progamming the child to give the right
answer, Papert urges that the most effective
learning occurs when the child can actually control
and program the language. Through the use of LOGO,
a language specifically designed to let children
program, children encounter very powerful ideas and
a new way of expressing mathematical thought and
phenomena.

Pask, Gordon, and Susan Curran. MICRO MAN:
COMPUTERS AND THE EVOLUTION OF CONSCIOUSNESS. New
York: Macmillan, 1982.

The developing relationship between computers and
humans is exmained for cooperative and antagonistic
elements. The authors hope that the two species
will learn to cooperate, leading to a
transformation in the humnan mind and the nature of
computing. Chapters discuss the history of
computers, threats posed by computers, language and
knowledge systems, applications of microprocessors,
computers and education, and the information
environment. Concludes with possible positive and
negative scenarios for the year 2000.

Peitchinis, S.G. COMPUTER TECHNOLOGY AND
EMPLOYMENT. New York: St. Martin's Press, 1983.

The Computer revolution is divided into three
phases. For the past 25 years we have seen the
first phase which involved the development of word
processing, computers, and copiers. In the next
phase, computers and telecommunications will merge
into telematic systems. The effects of both of
these phases on employment are considered positive.
A problematic effect, however, is predicted for the
third phases which will see the merging of
telematic systems of separate businesses and
institutions into one large network.

Piaget, J. THE CHILDREN'S CONCEPTION OF THE WORLD.
New York: Humanities, 1960.

Riedesel, C.A., and D.H. Clements. COPING WITH
COMPUTERS IN THE ELEMENTARY AND MIDDLE SCHOOLS.
Englewood Cliffs, New Jersey: Prentice-Hall, 1985.

Roberts, T.B. "States of Consciousness: A New
Inellectual Direction, A New Teacher Education
Direction." JOURNAL OF TEACHER EDUCATION 36
(March/April 1985):55-59.

Rotherman, Stanley, and Charles Mosmann. COMPUTERS
AND SOCIETY. 2nd ed. Chicago: Science Research
Associates, 1976.

Sanders, Donald. COMPUTERS IN SOCIETY. 2nd ed. New
York: McGraw-Hill, 1977.

Searle, John. "Minds, Brains, and Programs." THE
BEHAVIORAL AND BRAIN SCIENCES 3 (1980): 417-424.

Simon, S.B., L. Howe, and H. Kirschenbaum. VALUES
CLARIFICATION: A HANDBOOK OF PRACTICAL STRATEGIES
FOR TEACHERS AND STUDENTS. New York: Hart, 1978.

Tart, C.T. STATES OF CONSCIOUSNESS. New York: E.P.
Dutton, 1975.

Thornburg, D.D. "Artificial Intelligence." A+ 4
(March 1986): 55-59.

An introductory article into the world of
artificial intelligence which describes what has
been accomplished. Examples of expert systems are
provided as well as descriptions of the several
computer languages used to approximate artificial
intelligence.

Thornburg, D. BEYOND TURTLE GRAPHICS: FURTHER
EXPLORATIONS OF LOGO. Reading, Mass:
Addision-Wesley, 1986.

Thornburg, D.D. "A Computer Language at the
Crossroads: Logo." A+ 4 (March 1986): 78-84.

A review of the development of LOGO, including its
relationship to the symbol manipulation language
LISP. Reasons why LOGO has not become as widespread
a programming language as it should be are

explained. Finally, the benefits of learning LOGO
as a serious programming language are provided. The
author contends it offers much more that a
schoolchild's language.

Thornburg, D. DISCOVERING APPLE LOGO: AN INVITATION
TO THE ART AND PATTERN OF NATURE. Reading, Mass:
Addison-wesley, 1983.

Toffler, A. FUTURE SHOCK. New York: Random House,
1970.

Toffler, A. THE THIRD WAVE. New York: Charles E.
Merrill, 1980.

Turkle, S. THE SECOND SELF: COMPUTERS AND THE HUMAN
SPIRIT. New York: Simon and Schuster, 1984.

Using nativistic research techniques, such as
observation and interviews, the author collected
data on hundreds of subjects including young
children and computer experts. Looking at the
computer culture as a humanist, Turkel concludes
that working with the computer forces people to
confront the issue of whether they are "programmed"
or free. The coming of the computer parallels
another major philosophic inquiry earlier this
century, Freudian theory. Both of these phenomena
have in common the fact that they engaged humans in
self-reflection about our nature.

Watt, Dan. LEARNING WITH LOGO. New York:
McGraw-Hill, 1983.

Weil, A. THE NATURAL MIND: A NEW WAY OF LOOKING AT
DRUGS AND THE HIGHER CONSCIOUSNESS. Boston:
Houghton Mifflin, 1972.

Weizenbaum, Joseph. COMPUTER POWER AND HUMAN
REASON: FROM JUDGEMENT TO CALCULATION. San
Francisco: W.H. Freeman and Co., 1976.

Considered a classic in the field of artificial
intelligence by the author of the famous ELIZA
program, this book presents a brilliant analysis of
the similarities and differences in relation to how

humans think and computers operate. A critique of
the applications of artificial intelligence is
included.

Winston, P. ARTIFICIAL INTELLIGENCE. Reading, Mass:
Addison-Wesley, 1977.

AFTERWORD

About two weeks before I was to submit this manuscript to the publisher a development in educational computing came to my awareness that I felt was too important not to bring to the attention of social studies teachers. While this development is by no means complete the promise it holds for revolutionizing education cannot be underestimated. Jack Taub, the developer of a widely used information utility known as The Source, has turned his attention to providing a similar service for educational purposes to the classrooms of American schools. As Dennis Gooler, former Dean of the College of Education at Northern Illinois University, has noted, "The Education Utility has the potential to revitalize education and society." The following is a description of what the utility will provide and how it will work, once it is available for schools.

The Educational Utility will consist of the following elements. First, a repository of information including databases, reference materials such as encyclopedias and journals, textbooks from a variety of subject areas, and educational software programs of all kinds will be stored in computers of the National Information Utility, the company that will market Education Utility. This repository will be dynamic since users, publishers, and others can make arrangements to include additional offerings to the repository. This collection of information will represent an incredible amount of information and a heretofore unassembled and thus unavailable resource for teachers and learners.

A second component will be microcomputers located in individual classrooms, learning centers, and offices. Eventually, the goal will be to provide each student with a terminal, thus making individualized education feasible. Initially,

however, the Education Utility will appear in work
stations in a relatively small number of specially
designed classrooms and learning centers. The
microcomputer will be the means by which learners
will have access to the significant computing power
of the Utility itself.

The information stored in the national
computing system of the Education Utility will be
available on the following basis. Through
telecommunication linkups, such as a satellite
broadcast, information from the national computer,
called the Network Control Center, will be sent to
a state affiliate of the Utility where it can be
made available to a local district or school.
Transmissions can take place at non-peak times when
charges are lowest and then be available for
teacher and student use the next morning. Mr. Taub
is negotiating with AT&T to offer these
transmissions at a price that will be affordable by
schools. The preliminary figure reported by Taub
for the cost of accessing the Utility is below a
dollar an hour.

In addition to making massive amounts of
educational information directly available to
teachers and learners to be incorporated into
whatever instructional strategies are being used by
the teacher, the Utility will offer networking
possibilities. Thus, using features such as
electronic mail, students can interact with other
learners within a school, in any district, any
state, or even another country. A special teacher
work station that can be used to manage any
instruction provided to learners will be another
example of the networking possibilities. Similarly,
administrative work stations and links with home
stations are being planned. A final example of the
networking feature of the Utility involves revenue
generation. This will enable schools to sell to
individuals and interested businesses in the
community excess capacity on the Utility. By
selling non-school hours' time on the Utility to
interested parties, schools can help generate funds
to offset the costs associated with being a member
of the Utility.

In summary, the Education Utility will consist
of a massive and dynamic reservoir of information
and educational programming. Teacher and students
can plan instruction that will meet the individual

needs of the learner. Through the Utility, software
and textbook publishers will have an in-place
marketing and distribution system for any
educational materials they offer. How these
materials are used will still be under the direct
supervision of the classroom teacher, but the
teacher's responsibilities will shift to making
educationally sound decisions about what material
from the Utility to adopt for an individual
student. In short, once it is operational, the
Education Utility will be unique.

BIBLIOGRAPHY

Ferguson, Marilyn, "Education Utility Goal: 20,000
Classrooms by 1990." BRAIN/MIND BULLETIN 11
(February 10, 1986): 2-3.

Gooler, D.D. THE EDUCATION UTILITY: THE POWER TO
REVITALIZE EDUCATION AND SOCIETY. Englewood Cliffs,
N.J.: Education Technology Publications, 1986.

Social Studies Microcomputer Courseware Evaluation Guidelines

STEPHEN A. ROSE, ALLAN R. BRANDHORST, ALLEN D. GLENN, JAMES O. HODGES AND CHARLES S. WHITE

This document was produced by the Ad Hoc Committee on Computer Courseware Evaluation Guidelines for the National Council for the Social Studies. The authors are: Stephen A. Rose, Chairperson, University of Northern Iowa at Cedar Falls; Allan R. Brandhorst, University of South Carolina at Columbia; Allen D. Glenn, University of Minnesota at Minneapolis; James O. Hodges, Virginia Commonwealth University, Richmond; and Charles S. White, Indiana University at Bloomington.

Social studies educators at all levels are employing the microcomputer in a variety of instructional settings. Many social studies educators have little difficulty locating microcomputer hardware that can be used effectively in the classroom. Unfortunately, the same can not be said about courseware. ("software" designed for use in a course of study). While a multitude of educational courseware is available, identifying that courseware most useful for achieving social studies goals and objectives is often problematic. Even the existence of numerous generic courseware evaluation instruments has not made things easier, primarily because these instruments do not focus on the specific goals of the social studies. It was in response to this concern that the National Council for the Social Studies developed guidelines to evaluate and select social studies related courseware.

These guidelines contain three broad categories of questions—knowledge, skills and values. The implied criteria in the questions have been drawn from the "NCSS Social Studies Curriculum Guidelines," "Curriculum Guidelines for Multiethnic Education," and "Essentials of the Social Studies." Collectively, these documents outline a variety of roles the social studies play in preparing youth for full participation in society. Social studies, for example, should specify goals that go beyond the acquisition of academic content and seek to develop learners who have the personal, social and intellectual skills needed for both citizenship and effective participation in society. Moreover, it is essential that social studies programs have students develop a realistic picture of themselves, examine their own values and value systems, and increase their reading, writing, thinking and speaking skills. Additionally, the social studies curriculum should help students understand and appreciate cultural diversity throughout the world and develop the capacities for working cooperatively with others. Lastly, social studies education is directly concerned with the development of students' understanding of the body of knowledge developed and refined by historians and social scientists. This includes important facts, concepts, generalizations and skills that permit students to explain and describe social phenomena affecting their lives.

Computer courseware materials must be evaluated carefully in two stages. First, educators need to determine whether or not a particular set of materials is appropriate for use in the social studies classroom. These guidelines address that need: they contain criteria derived from the goals and purposes most appropriate to social studies. Second, while judging the value of a set of computer courseware as it relates to the goals of social studies, educators must also confront technical and instructional issues. There are many excellent evaluation guidelines already available for this purpose, including the *Evaluator's Guide to Microcomputer Based Instructional Packages* published by MicroSift and *Guidelines for Evaluating Computerized Instructional Materials* by the National Council of Teachers of Mathematics. These and other such evaluation instruments are identified at the end of this document.

The two-stage evaluation process described above, with one stage focusing on the courseware's relationship to the overall goals of the social studies and the other on the technical/instructional issues, is an integral process. By assuring that both stages receive careful attention, the social studies educator should be able to determine whether a particular set of computer courseware should be used, and if so, where and how. The final goal is the selection of computer courseware that meets the instructional goals and objectives of a particular social studies teacher.

SOCIAL STUDIES MICROCOMPUTER COURSEWARE EVALUATION GUIDELINES

The guidelines are organized around three areas—*Knowledge, Skills,* and *Values*—each of which contains organizational descriptors. A checklist has been included to help evaluators monitor the extent of emphasis a courseware package places on each criterion. The checklist contains four headings—Strong Emphasis (SE), Moderate Emphasis (ME), Inadequate Emphasis (IE), and Not Applicable (NA). When using the checklist, it is important to realize that the breadth of criteria in this document and the variety of courseware on the market preclude a single courseware package from meeting all the standards in these guidelines.

Knowledge

Social studies educators at all levels have rejected a curricula based exclusively on the behavioral and social sciences. Instead, they have adopted a broad-based curriculum that not only addresses the concerns of those academic disciplines but concentrates on the personal and social concerns of the student, as well as the multicultural and normative concerns of society.

SE	ME	IE	NA	
				Significant Characteristics
				1.01 Validity
				Does the courseware emphasize currently valid knowledge from one or more of the social sciences?*
				1.02 Accuracy
				Does the courseware present a true and comprehensive body of content, free of distortion by omission?
				1.03 Reality Oriented
				Does the courseware's content deal with the realities of today's world in terms of its flaws, strengths, dangers and promises?
				1.04 Significance of Past and Present
				Does the courseware deal with important concepts, principles and theories of modern society? Does it present significant ideas that convey the excitement of the past, present and future?
				1.05 Bias
				Does the courseware avoid bias and/or stereotyping with regard to gender, ethnicity, racial background, religious application or cultural group? When unfamiliar customs and institutions or different ethnic groups and cultures are dealt with, are they presented in an unbiased and objective manner?
				Content Emphasis
				1.11 Issue Analysis
				Does the courseware engage students in analyzing and attempting to resolve social issues? Is a data base provided and does it contain information of sufficient depth and breadth for students to make realistic decisions? If not, can the data base be expanded by the teacher or student?

SE	ME	IE	NA	
				1.12 Pervasive and Enduring Issues
				Does the courseware focus on problems and/or issues that are socially significant? Do the materials demonstrate the reciprocal relationships among the social sciences, social issues and action?
				1.13 Global Perspectives
				Does the courseware help students develop a global perspective? Are students assisted in recognizing the local, national and global implications of the problems being examined and their possible solutions?
				1.14 Development of Society
				Does the courseware develop knowledge and insights into the historical development of human society? Do the facts, concepts, principles and processes presented offer direction in organizing a study of human behavior? Does it help students understand: how modern societies develop, the role of central institutions and values of national societies and those of the world community?
				1.15 Multiculturalism
				Does the courseware help develop an understanding of the diversity of cultures and institutional arrangements within American society and in other societies within the global community? Does it provide a rational explanation for customs and other distinctive aspects of daily life arrangements that are explored? Does it contribute to the students' acceptance of the legitimacy of their own cultural identity as well as that of others?
				1.16 Personal/Social Growth
				Does the courseware help students understand their own development and capabilities, as influenced by their families, peer groups, ethnic groups, media, and the society at large?

*History is included in this classification.

Skills

Social studies education should provide students with the opportunities to develop, practice, and use a variety of thought processes and skills. Students should have opportunities to probe, to extract knowledge from experience, to think and to communicate their findings and conclusions, both orally and in writing. They should learn how to learn—to develop self-direction in gaining meaningful knowledge and employing it effectively. The social studies program should develop the student's ability to make rational decisions. In order to accomplish this, it is essential that students acquire skills in critical thinking, inquiry, information processing and problem solving.

SE	ME	IE	NA			SE	ME	IE	NA	

Intellectual Skills

2.01 Inquiry and Problem Solving
Does the courseware pose problems which require students to use the methods of inquiry? Specifically, are students given practice in: identifying and defining problems, formulating and testing hypotheses, and arriving at valid generalizations?

2.02 Critical Thinking
Does the courseware foster the development of critical thinking skills of distinguishing between fact and opinion, detecting slant and bias, determining cause and effect, and evaluating mining the reliability of sources?

2.03 Higher Cognitive Levels
Does the courseware help students develop and/or reinforce the thought processes of analysis, synthesis and evaluation? Do students encounter material that helps develop their understanding of the relationship between elements and how these elements fit together as a whole? Are students given opportunities to use information to construct a new communication? Are students asked to make judgments based on appropriate criteria?

2.04 Divergent Thinking
Does the courseware encourage divergent thinking which allows students to provide a variety of answers for difficult questions?

2.05 Concept Formation
Does the courseware present a broad range of illustrations, models, and examples which are appropriate for helping students image, dissect, conceptualize, define, or recognize relationships between patterns or concepts?

Decisionmaking Skills

2.11 Processes
Does the courseware develop decisionmaking skills of identifying alternatives, establishing criteria to evaluate the alternatives, evaluating the alternatives in light of criteria and making the decisions? Are students given the opportunity to re-test, re-interpret and re-organize their beliefs about facts and values?

2.12 Learning Environment
Does the courseware and its accompanying materials create a social environment populated by believable characters confronting difficult circumstances and choices?

2.13 Choices
Does the courseware require the student to make choices, and are those choices then used as data for reflection?

2.14 Information Base
Does the courseware's data match the kind of data that would be accessible by citizens outside the instructional context? Is the courseware flexible enough to allow the alteration and addition of information, so that students can practice making decisions under a variety of factual and value circumstances?

2.15 Consequences
Does the courseware confront students with realistic consequences (for themselves and for others) of decisions they are required to make in using the courseware?

2.16 Assessment
Does the courseware and its accompanying materials assist the teacher and the student to assess the latter's skills and abilities in decisionmaking?

2.17 Degree of Certainty
Does the courseware provide experiences in making decisions under conditions of uncertainty? Does the courseware help the student recall the basis on which decisions were made and to make revised decisions informed by new understandings?

Information Processing Skills

2.21 Orientation Skills
Does the courseware foster the development of map and globe skills?

2.22 Chronology and Time Skills
Does the courseware provide students practice in interpreting chronology and applying time skills, i.e., sequencing events and trends, and identifying and using measures of time correctly?

2.23 Graphic Data Skills
Does the courseware help students develop skills of reading and interpreting, constructing and drawing inferences from graphs, tables and charts?

2.24 Gathering and Processing Data
Does the courseware provide opportunities for students to develop skills in locating, organizing, interpreting and presenting data?

2.25 Content Reading Skills
Does the courseware facilitate the development of the student's word attack skills and the ability to read on the literal, intepretative and applied levels?

2.26 Communication Skills
Does the courseware or its accompanying materials foster adequately developed communication skills and provide opportunities for communicating effectively orally and in writing?

Cooperation and Participation Skills

2.31 Interaction
Does the courseware and its accompanying materials require groups of students to work together? Do the learning tasks require a division of labor? Does successful completion of

SE	ME	IE	NA	
				the tasks require shared information?
				2.32 Cooperation
				Does the courseware and its accompanying materials reinforce the importance of, and provide support for, cooperation in resolving conflicts over contradictory facts and values?
				2.33 Social/Political Participation
				Does interaction with the courseware and its accompanying materials enhance the student's ability to participate effectively in the social and political processes of his/her school and community?
				2.34 Follow-up Activities
				Does the courseware or its accompanying material offer suggestions for activities that follow logically from the use of the courseware? Does the courseware allow students to experience vicariously the positive and negative consequences, the costs and benefits, the frustrations and satisfactions of taking action?

Values

The cultural pluralism characterizing American society makes value conflicts inevitable. These conflicts are particularly evident in debates about solutions to complex social problems confronting our society. Effective participation in resolving these problems requires people who have rationally developed their own value system, and who are proficient at making defensible value decisions.

Social studies education should provide ample opportunities for students to rationally examine value issues in a non-indoctrinating environment. Additionally, it should promote the reflective examination of value dilemmas that underlie the personal and social issues that students confront in their everyday lives.

SE	ME	IE	NA	
				Societal Orientation
				3.01 Influence of Values on Behavior
				Does the courseware help students develop an understanding and appreciation of the influence of beliefs and values on human behavior patterns?
				3.02 Procedural Values
				Does the courseware help the student identify and develop an appreciation for values that underlie substantive beliefs and procedural guarantees expressed in this nation's fundamental documents?
				Valuing Processes
				3.11 Beliefs
				Does the courseware require the student to identify his or her own beliefs, to make choices based on those beliefs, and to understand the consequences of the choices made?
				3.12 Conjoint Reflection
				Does the courseware require conjoint

				reflection on feelings, behaviors and beliefs?
				3.13 Defensible Judgments
				Does the courseware support a process of value analysis by which learners can make rational, defensible value judgments?
				3.14 Feedback
				Does the courseware track the process students use in making value judgments and provide useful feedback with respect to its quality and improvement?

SYSTEMS FOR EVALUATING TECHNICAL AND INSTRUCTIONAL COURSEWARE ISSUES

Computer Library Media Consortium for Classroom Evaluation of Microcomputer Courseware, 1983. San Mateo County Office of Education, 333 Main Street, Redwood City, CA 94073. Phone (415) 363-5400. (A three-page untitled evaluation reporting form.)

Dennis, J. Richard. *Evaluating Materials for Teaching with a Computer,* includes "Courseware Evaluation Worksheet." The Illinois Series on Educational Application of Computers, No. 5e, Department of Secondary Education, University of Illinois at Urbana-Champaign, 1979.

Douglas, Shirley and Gary Neights. *A Guide to Instructional Microcomputer Software,* includes "Microcomputer Software Evaluation Form." Instructional Materials Service Programs, Pennsylvania Department of Education, Box 911, 333 Market Street, Harrisburg, PA 17108. Phone (717) 783-2528.

Evaluating Instructional Computer Courseware; Materials Review and Education Center, Division of Educational Media, Department of Public Instruction, Raleigh, NC.

Evaluation Guide for Microcomputer-Based Instructional Packages. Developed by MicroSift, The Computer Technology Program, Northwest Regional Educational Laboratory. Published by International Council for Computers in Education, Dept. of Computer and Information Science, University of Oregon, 1982.

Heck, William P. et al. *Guidelines for Evaluating Computerized Instructional Materials.* The National Council for Teachers of Mathematics, Inc., Reston, VA, 1981.

Rosenstock, Robert, Norman Dodl and John Burton. *Education Microware Assessment: Criteria and Procedures for Evaluating Instructional Software.* Education Microcomputer Laboratory, Room 400, War Memorial Gym, Virginia Tech, Blacksburg, VA 24061. Phone (703) 961-5587.

Smith, Richard A. (ed.). *Guidelines for Software Evaluation,* Department of Technology, Houston Independent School District, Houston, TX (a four-page questionnaire).

◼ SOFTWARE EVALUATION CHECKLIST

PROGRAM NAME: _____ SOURCE: _____ COST: _____

SUBJECT AREA: _____ REVIEWER'S NAME: _____ DATE: _____

1. INSTRUCTIONAL RANGE

_____ grade level(s)

_____ ability level(s)

2. INSTRUCTIONAL GROUPING FOR PROGRAM USE

_____ individual

_____ small group (size: _____)

_____ large group (size: _____)

3. EXECUTION TIME

_____ minutes (estimated) for average use

4. PROGRAM USE(S)

_____ drill or practice

_____ tutorial

_____ simulation

_____ instructional gaming

_____ problem solving

_____ informational

_____ other (_____)

5. USER ORIENTATION: INSTRUCTOR'S POINT OF VIEW

low						high	
•	•	•	•	•	•	flexibility	
•	•	•	•	•	•	freedom from need to intervene or assist	

6. USER ORIENTATION: STUDENT'S POINT OF VIEW

low						high	
•	•	•	•	•	•	quality of directions (clarity)
•	•	•	•	•	•	quality of output (content and tone)
•	•	•	•	•	•	quality of screen formatting
•	•	•	•	•	•	freedom from need for external information
•	•	•	•	•	•	freedom from disruption by system errors
•	•	•	•	•	•	simplicity of user input

7. CONTENT

low					high	
•	•	•	•	•	•	instructional focus
•	•	•	•	•	•	instructional significance
•	•	•	•	•	•	soundness or validity
•	•	•	•	•	•	compatibility with other materials used

8. MOTIVATION AND INSTRUCTIONAL STYLE

passive					active	
•	•	•	•	•	•	type of student involvement

low					high	
•	•	•	•	•	•	degree of student control

none	poor				good	
•	•	•	•	•	•	use of game format
•	•	•	•	•	•	use of still graphics
•	•	•	•	•	•	use of animation
•	•	•	•	•	•	use of color
•	•	•	•	•	•	use of voice input and output
•	•	•	•	•	•	use of nonvoice audio
•	•	•	•	•	•	use of light pen
•	•	•	•	•	•	use of ancillary materials
•	•	•	•	•	•	use of _____

9. SOCIAL CHARACTERISTICS

present and negative	not present	present and positive	
_____	_____	_____	competition
_____	_____	_____	cooperation
_____	_____	_____	humanizing of computer
_____	_____	_____	moral issues or value judgments
_____	_____	_____	summary of student performance

1. The grade levels and ability levels for a particular program are primarily determined by the concepts involved. Other important factors are reading level, prerequisite skills, degree of student control, and intended instructional use. It is possible for a program to be flexible enough to be used across a wide range of grade levels and ability levels.

2. Some programs are designed for use by individuals. Others have been or can be modified for participation by two or three persons at a time. Simulations or demonstrations often pose opportunities for large-group interaction. A given program may be used in more than one grouping, depending on the instructor.

3. The time required for the use of a program will vary considerably. Include loading time for cassettes. A time range is the appropriate response here.

4. Instructional programs can be categorized according to their uses. Some programs may have more than one use, thus falling into more than one of the following categories:

Drill or practice: Assumes that the concept or skill has been taught previously.

Tutorial: Directs the full cycle of the instructional process; a dialogue between the student and the computer.

Simulation: Models selected, alterable aspects of an environment.

Instructional gaming: Involves random events and the pursuit of a winning strategy.

Problem solving: Uses general algorithms common to one or more problems.

Informational: Generates information (data).

5. These are factors relevant to the actual use of the program from the point of view of an instructor.

Flexibility: A program may allow the user or the instructor to adjust the program to different ability levels, degrees of difficulty, or concepts.

Intervention or assistance: A rating of "low" means considerable teacher intervention or assistance is required.

6. These are factors relevant to the actual use of the program from the point of view of a student.

Directions: The directions should be complete, readable, under the user's control (e.g., should not scroll off the screen until understood), and use appropriate examples.

Output: Program responses should be readable, understandable, and complete. If in response to student input, the output should be of an acceptable tone and consistent with the input request.

Screen formatting: The formats during a program run should not be distracting or cluttered. Labels and symbols should be meaningful within the given context.

External information: A program may require the user to have access to information other than that provided within it. This may include prerequisite content knowledge or knowledge of conventions used by the program designer as well as maps, books, models, and so on.

System errors: System errors result in the involuntary termination of the program.

Input: A program should ensure that a user knows when and in what form input is needed. It should avoid using characters with special meanings, restrict input locations to particular screen areas, and require minimal typing.

7. These are matters relevant to the subject-matter content of the program.

Focus: The program topic should be clearly defined and of a scope that permits thorough treatment.

Significance: The instructional objectives of the program must be viewed as important by the instructor. Also, the program should represent a valid use of the computer's capabilities while improving the instructional process.

Soundness or validity: The concepts and terms employed should be correct, clear, and precise. Other important factors are the rate of presentation, degree of difficulty, and internal consistency.

Compatibility: The content, terminology, teaching style, and educational philosophy of the program should be consistent with those generally encountered by the student.

9. Competition, cooperation, and values are concerns that may be a function of the way a program expresses them. (War gaming and the "hangman" format are sample issues.) Also, the "humanizing" of the computer may serve for motivation or to reduce anxiety, but it also may become tedious, misleading, and counterproductive.

The summary of student performance can be dichotomous (win or lose), statistical (time expended or percent of items correct), or subjective (as in the evaluation of a simulation). It may be for student, teacher, or both.

SAMPLE CITATIONS FROM FOUR SOCIAL STUDIES-RELATED DATABASES:
America: History and Life; Historical Abstracts; ERIC; Magazine Index

File 38:America: History & Life - 63-84/Iss21A2
(Copr. ABC Clio Inc.)
```
    Set Items Description
    ‾‾‾ ‾‾‾‾‾ ‾‾‾‾‾‾‾‾‾‾‾
              4 NUCLEAR TECHNOLOGY
              1 NUCLEAR WARFARE
         S1   5 NUCLEAR TECHNOLOGY OR NUCLEAR WARFARE
```

? T1/5/1-3
1/5/1
        426410   15A-04710
        ATOMS FOR BRAZIL, DANGER FOR ALL.
        Gall, Norman Gall, Norman.
        Foreign Policy 1976 (23): 155-201.
        Document Type: ARTICLE
        West Germany's agreement to provide Brazil with the largest transfer
of nuclear technology ever given a developing country is an initial step
in worldwide nuclear proliferation. US readiness in the past to provide
nuclear technology to both its allies and to private American corporations
dictates that the technology is available to almost any country willing
to pay the high price. One solution to eliminate competition and provide
controls would be an international confederation of suppliers which through
its directorate could set the standards and controls for peaceful nuclear
development. Primary and secondary sources; 54 notes (C. Hopkins)
        Descriptors: USA; 1945-1976; Brazil; Germany, West; Nuclear Technology,
Transfer of

1/5/2
        422849   15A-01284
        BEGINNINGS OF DEVELOPMENT IN NUCLEAR TECHNOLOGY.
        Hewlett, Richard G Hewlett, Richard G.
        Technology and Culture 1976 17(3): 465-478.
        Document Type: ARTICLE
        In both the Manhattan Project and the early Atomic Energy Commission,
tension arose between the scientists, who wished to keep charge of the projects
they had begun, and the engineers, who were better able to bring them to
fruition. The "engineer is better qualified both technically and psycholog-
ically than the scientist to determine when the change of command should
occur." Based on published works by the authors; 23 notes. (C. O. Smith)
        Descriptors: 1938-1950; Nuclear Technology; Manhattan Project; Atomic
Energy Commission; Scientists; Engineers

1/5/3
        386432   14A-06254
        NUCLEAR POLICY SHOULD BE MORE OPEN AND LESS AMBIGUOUS.
        Legault, Albert Legault, Albert.
        Internat. Perspectives (Canada) 1976 (1): 8-13.
        Document Type: ARTICLE
        Discusses the need for less government secrecy about Canada's supplying
nuclear technology to India and other nations, 1968-70's, emphasizing the
implications of the Treaty on the Non-Proliferation of Nuclear Weapons (1968).
        Descriptors: 1968-1970's; Government secrecy; Canada; Nuclear technology;
India; Nuclear Nonproliferation Treaty - (1968)

-2-

File 39:Historical Abstracts - 73-84/Iss35B2
(Copr. ABC Clio Inc.)
    Set Items Description
? S NUCLEAR WAR OR TECHNOLOGY
            3 NUCLEAR WAR
         2124 TECHNOLOGY
     2 2127 NUCLEAR WAR OR TECHNOLOGY
? S NUCLEAR WAR OR NUCLEAR POWER
            3 NUCLEAR WAR
           41 NUCLEAR POWER
     3   44 NUCLEAR WAR OR NUCLEAR POWER
? S NUCLEAR WAR
        4   3 NUCLEAR WAR
? T4/5/1-3
4/5/1
    1064067   34B-05871
    NATO'S FIRST USE DOCTRINE: BACKGROUND, REMONSTRANCES, AND REFLECTIONS
    NATOS FORSTEBRUKSDOKTRINE: BACKGRUNN, INNVENDINGER OG ETTERTANKE
    Skogan, John Kristen
    Int. Pol. (Norway) 1982 (1B): 141-171.
    Document Type: ARTICLE
    Languages: Norwegian.
    After a survey of nuclear doctrine developments within NATO, discusses
objections, expostulations, and arguments than can and have been raised
regarding the current NATO first use posture, pointing out advantages.

4/5/2
    766069   22B-00063
    THE PREVENTION OF NUCLEAR WAR IN A WORLD OF UNCERTAINTY.
    Ikle, Fred C Ikle, Fred C.
    Foreign Service J. 1974 51(5): 10-12, 30.
    Document Type: ARTICLE
    Adapted from a speech before the joint Harvard/MIT Arms Control Seminar.
(S)
    Descriptors: 1945-1974; Nuclear war, prevention of; Arms Control

4/5/3
    719332   21B-03109
    FORGETTING ABOUT THE UNTHINKABLE.
    Paarlberg, Rob Paarlberg, Rob.
    Foreign Policy 1973 (10): 132-140.
    Document Type: ARTICLE
    Discusses the loss of public interest in the prospect of nuclear war.
(S)
    Descriptors: Public Opinion; 1945-1971; Nuclear War

-3-

File *1:ERIC - 66-84/Oct
        Set Items Description

     130 NUCLEAR TECHNOLOGY (APPLICATION AND USE OF NUCLEA
     249 NUCLEAR WARFARE
S3   361 NUCLEAR TECHNOLOGY OR NUCLEAR WARFARE

3/5/1
EJ300578   SO512846
     A NUCLEAR ARMS RACE UNIT.
     Totten, Sam
     Social Studies, v75 n3 p102-05 May-Jun   1984
     Available from: UMI
     Language: English
     Document Type: TEACHING GUIDE (052)
     Including both social studies and language skills objectives, this
unit of study encourages senior high school students to examine and wrestle
with issues concerning nuclear warfare. Activities suggested are many and
varied, e.g., students read and discuss fiction and nonfiction, analyze
films, do library work, write essays, and conduct surveys. (RM)
     Descriptors: *Disarmament; *English Instruction; High Schools; *Inter-
disciplinary Approach; Learning Activities; *Nuclear Warfare; Peace; *Social
Studies; Units of Study; World Problems

3/5/2
ED240046   SO015424
     CROSSROADS: QUALITY OF LIFE IN A NUCLEAR WORLD. A HIGH SCHOOL SOCIAL
STUDIES CURRICULUM.
     French, Dan; And Others
     Jobs with Peace, Boston, MA.
     1983 87p.; For related documents, see SO 015 422-423. Several photographs
and resources with small type may not reproduce clearly.
     Available from: Jobs with Peace, 77 Summer St., Room 1111, Boston,
MA 02110 ($4.00 per unit, $10.00 per set of three units in English, science,
and social studies).
     EDRS Price - MF01 Plus Postage. PC Not Available from EDRS.
     Language: English
     Document Type: TEACHING GUIDE (052)
     Geographic Source: U.S.; Massachusetts
     Journal Announcement: RIEJUN84
     One of a set of high school curricula on nuclear issues, this 10-day
social studies unit helps students understand the interrelationship of economics, the arms race, military spending, and the threat of nuclear war. Activities such as role plays, discussion, brainstorming, and problem solving
develop students' abilities to evaluate issues and information in order
to make educated decisions. Topics covered in the 10 lessons are conflict
and resolution, war and negotiation, countries currently at war, effects
of a nuclear explosion, Hiroshima, perceptions of the Soviet Union, and
the quality of life. In a culminating activity, students are encouraged
to express their feelings and explore ways they can affect society. Each
lesson includes a plan sheet, readings, students activities, worksheets,
and a homework assignment. Additional materials include an evaluation form;
a bibliography; and lists of informational, instructional, and audiovisual
materials. (LP)
     Descriptors: Budgets; Civil Defense; Conflict Resolution; Controversial
Issues (Course Content); Disarmament; Economic Factors; Foreign Countries;
Foreign Policy; High Schools; Instructional Materials; *International Problem
Solving; Quality of Life; Role Playing; Skill Development; Social Studies;
Taxes; Units of Study; War; *World Problems
     Identifiers: Japan (Hiroshima)

-4-

File 47:MAGAZINE INDEX - 1959-March 1970, 1973-84/Oct
(Copr. IAC) FMT 9 - $7.00
        Set Items Description? .Execute T4JV
                11 NUCLEAR TECHNOLOGY
                3 NUCLEAR WARFARE
        S1   14   NUCLEAR TECHNOLOGY OR NUCLEAR WARFARE

?T1/5/1-5
1/5/1
1592363   DATABASE: MI File 47
    A matter of visibility.
    Macleans   v96   p62(1)   April 25   1983
    CODEN: MCNMB
    DESCRIPTORS: moving-pictures, documentary-television use; If You Love
This Planet (moving-picture)-television use; nuclear warfare-television
use.

1/5/2
0837884   DATABASE: MI File 47
    Nuclear power: an energetic debate.
    Galbreath, Beth L.
    Christian Century   v93   p897   Oct 20   1976
    DESCRIPTORS: Nuclear energy.; Nuclear warfare-Survival.

1/5/3
0826406   DATABASE: MI File 47
    Nuclear energy debates: liberation or development?
    Maxey, Margaret N.
    Christian Century   v93   p656   Jul 21   1976
    DESCRIPTORS: Nuclear energy-Hazards.; Nuclear energy-Moral aspects.;
Nuclear warfare-Survival.; National Council of Churches.

1/5/4
0825611   DATABASE: MI File 47
    Nuclear proliferation (I): warnings from the arms control community.
    Hammand, Allen L.
    Science   v193   p126   Jul 9   1976
    DESCRIPTORS: Nuclear weapons and disarmament.; Nuclear technology-Laws
and regulations.; Uranium-Enrichment.

1/5/5
0793710   DATABASE: MI FILE 47
    The nuclear nightmare V. A tragic paradox.
    Stockholm, Sweden. International Peace Research Institute.
    UNESCO Courier   p29   Nov   1975
    DESCRIPTORS: Nuclear technology-Military applications.

DATABASES FOR SOCIAL STUDIES EDUCATION

A-V ONLINE (formerly NICES), current, 403,000 records, irregular updates (National Information Center for Educational Media, Access Innovations, Inc., Albuquerque, NM)

A-V ONLINE offers comprehensive coverage of non-print educational material: A-V ONLINE covers the entire spectrum of the educational field from pre-school to professional and graduate school levels. Librarians, media specialists, curriculum planners, and researchers who search A-V ONLINE will gain references to all types of educational media—16mm films, 35mm filmstrips, overhead transparencies, audio tapes, video tapes, phonograph records, motion picture cartridges, and slides.

$70 per online connect hour, 20¢ per full record printed offline. (DIALOG File 46)

EDUCATIONAL RESOURCES INFORMATION CENTER (ERIC), 1966-present, monthly updates (ERIC Processing and Reference Facility, 4833 Rugby Avenue, Suite 301, Bethesda, MD 20814)

ERIC contains approximately half a million citations covering research findings, project and technical reports, speeches, unpublished manuscripts, books, and journal articles in the field of education. Educators, academicians, administrators, and researchers will all find ERIC a key source for educational information. Citations include detailed source, geographic, institutional, and availability information in addition to ERIC subject descriptors and extensive abstracts.

$25 per online connect hour, 10¢ per full record printed offline. (BRS and DIALOG)

RESOURCES IN COMPUTER EDUCATION (RICE), 1979-present, updated every other month (Northwest Regional Educational Laboratory, 300 SW Sixth Avenue, Portland, OR 97204)

RICE is geared toward providing a reference and registry service for school districts, educational agencies, and other educational institutions. The database is comprised of a variety of information on the state of the art in educational computer applications. Citations include references to educational software packages and their producers, featuring detailed software and hardware requirement data, product descriptions and evaluations, information on intended end-user/audience and further instructional information. (BRS)

SCHOOL PRACTICES INFORMATION FILE (SPIF), products, programs, or materials currently in operation or use, monthly updates (BRS, 1200 Route 7, Latham, NY 12110)

SPIF contains descriptions of educational practices, programs, tests, materials, and products that are currently in operation or use. Subject areas covered include special education, inservice education, basic skills, school business practices, and curriculum development. Grade level, target audience, evaluative comment, resource type, and availability information accompanies SPIF records. This database is valuable to all professionals concerned with educational practices. (BRS)

AMERICA: HISTORY AND LIFE, 1964-present, 194,000 records, updated 3 times
per year (ABC-Clio Information Services, Santa Barbara, CA)

AMERICA: HISTORY AND LIFE (AHL), covering the full range of U.S. and
Canadian history, area studies, and current affairs, is a comprehensive
and current aid to bibliographic research. The online database corresponds
to the printed America: History and Life, Part A (Article Abstracts and
Citations), Part B (Index to Book Reviews), and Part C (American History
Bibliography).

AHL includes coverage for the following typical areas: American studies,
ethnic studies, folklore, history, historiography and methodology, international
relations, local history, oral history, prehistory, politics and government,
popular culture, teaching of history, and urban affairs.

$65 per online connect hour, 15¢ full record printed offline. (DIALOG
File 38)

DRUGINFO AND ALCOHOL USE AND ABUSE (DRUG, DRSC, HAZE), 1968-present, quarterly
updates (Drug Information Service [DIS], College of Pharmacy, University
of Minnesota, Minneapolis, MN 55455)

Social workers, therapists, social scientists, educators, and information
specialists will find these three interrelated databases of use. DRUGINFO
(DRSC) covers the educational, sociological, and psychological aspects of
alcohol and drug use and abuse. Alcohol Use and Abuse (HAZE) includes material
on treatment evaluation, chemical dependence, family therapy, the MMPI,
and alcoholism among various populations. DRUG represents a concatena-
tion of these two files. All three databases include references to articles,
reprints, monographs, pamphlets, conference papers, instructional guides,
and films. Every citation identifies study type and level, and includes
concise abstracts. (BRS)

HISTORICAL ABSTRACTS, 1973-present, 178,300 records, quarterly updates (ABC-
Clio Information Services, Santa Barbara, CA)

HISTORICAL ABSTRACTS is a reference service that abstracts and indexes
the world's periodical literature in history and the related social sciences
and humanities. The database corresponds to the two companion publications,
Historical Abstracts Part A, Modern History Abstracts (1450-1914); and Historical Abstracts Part B, Twentieth-Century Abstracts (1914 to the present).
HISTORICAL ABSTRACTS covers the history of the world from 1450 to the present,
excluding the U.S. and Canada, which are covered by AMERICA: HISTORY AND
LIFE (File 38). Articles are abstracted from more than 2,000 journals published
in 90 countries in some 30 languages.

$65 per online connect hour, 15¢ per full record printed offline. (DIALOG
File 39)

SOCIAL SCISEARCH, 1972-present, 1,364,000 records, monthly updates (Institute
for Scientific Information, Philadelphia, PA)

SOCIAL SCISEARCH is a multidisciplinary database indexing every significant item from the 1,500 most important social sciences journals throughout
the world and social sciences articles selected from 3,000 additional journals
in the natural, physical, and biomedical sciences. The SOCIAL SCISEARCH
includes many important monographs as well. SOCIAL SCISEARCH covers every
area of the social and behavioral sciences. It corresponds to the printed
Social Science Citation Index.

-3-

SOCIAL SCISEARCH offers a unique information retrieval technique. In addition to more conventional retrieval by title words or phrases, source authors, journal names, corporate source, etc., it is also possible to search by way of the author's cited references.

Subscribers to the ISI print indexes receive a reduced rate when searching SOCIAL SCISEARCH on DIALOG.

SDI: $5.95 (subs); $6.95 (nonsubs)/update

$110 per online connect hour, 20¢ per full record printed offline (nonsubscribers); $75 per online connect hour, 15¢ per full record printed offline (subscribers). (DIALOG File 7)

UNITED STATES POLITICAL SCIENCE DOCUMENTS, 1975-present, 24,500 records, quarterly updates (NASA Industrial Applications Center, University of Pittsburgh, Pittsburgh, PA)

USPSD provides detailed abstracts and indexing from approximately 150 of the major American journals pubishing scholarly articles in the broad area of political science. Coverage includes such specific areas as foreign policy, international relations, behavioral sciences, public administration, economics, law and contemporary problems, world politics, and all areas of political science including theory and methodology. This database is of particular interest to the academic community in providing a central source from which to access significant research results in the political, social, and policy sciences.

$65 per online connect hour, 15¢ per full record printed offline. (DIALOG File 93)

FACTS ON FILE, 1982-present, 3,500 records, weekly updates, (Facts on File, Inc., New York, NY)

FACTS ON FILE is a weekly record of contemporary history compiled from worldwide news sources. It covers politics, government, business and the economy, medicine, sports, foreign affairs, the arts, and other news topics. FACTS ON FILE contains news summaries which are both comprehensive and concise, highlighting the factual content in news stories. This file can be used for tracing developments in important and interesting news stories. FACTS ON FILE corresponds to the printed Facts on File.

$60 per online connect hour, 25¢ per full record printed offline. (DIALOG File 264)

MAGAZINE ASAP^{TM}, 1983-present, 10,000 records, monthly updates (Information Access Company, Belmont, CA)

MAGAZINE ASAP provides the complete text and indexing for over 50 publications selected from the approximately 400 publications covered in MAGAZINE INDEX. The full text of each article is searchable, and complete articles may be received online. MAGAZINE ASAP includes not only the complete text of articles, but also of editorials, columns, reviews, product evaluation, and recipes.

$84 per online connect hour, $7.00 per full record printed offline or typed or displayed online (Format 9) (DIALOG File 647)

-4-

MAGAZINE INDEX^TM, 1959 to March 1970, 1973-present, 1,468,000 records, monthly updates (Information Access Company, Belmont, CA)

MAGAZINE INDEX is the first online database to offer truly broad coverage of general interest magazines. This database was created especially for general reference, to handle a constant flow of diverse requests for information from the scholarly to the light hearted. MAGAZINE INDEX covers more than 435 popular magazines and provides extensive coverage of current affairs, the performing arts, business, sports, recreation and travel, consumer product evaluations, science and technology, leisure time activities, and other areas. In addition to general reference, MAGAZINE INDEX will serve businesses and government libraries with information not available on any other online database. Users in the fields of market research, public relations, government relations, journalism, food and nutrition, and the social sciences will find MAGAZINE INDEX to be a significant resource. In addition to its extensive indexing, MAGAZINE INDEX contains the full text of records from more than 50 magazines from 1983 to the present.

$84 per online connect hour, 20¢ per full record (Format 5) printed offline, 10¢ per full record (Format 5) typed or displayed online; $7.00 per Format 9 record printed offline or typed or displayed online. [Note: Format 9 contains the complete text of articles.] (DIALOG File 47)

NEWSEARCH^TM, current month only, 1,200-54,000 records, daily updates (Information Access Company, Belmont, CA)

NEWSEARCH is a daily index of more than 2,000 news stories, information articles, and book reviews from over 1,700 of the most important newspapers, magazines, and periodicals. In addition to these publications, NEWSEARCH also includes the full text of PR Newswire (which is transferred to TRADE AND INDUSTRY INDEX monthly). Every working day the previous day's news stories are indexed and added to NEWSEARCH to provide current information on general news; product reviews; executive and corporation news; current events; book, record, theatre reviews; business and trade news; and much more. At the end of each month the magazine article data is transferred to the MAGAZINE INDEX database (File 74); the newspaper indexing data is transferred to the NATIONAL NEWSPAPER INDEX database (File 111). Indexing for LEGAL RESOURCE INDEX (File 150), MANAGEMENT CONTENTS (File 75), and TRADE AND INDUSTRY INDEX (File 148) is also transferred at the end of each month.

$120 per online connect hour, 20¢ per full record printed offline. (DIALOG File 211)

NATIONAL NEWSPAPER INDEX^TM, 1979-present, (1982-present for the Los Angeles Times and the Washington Post), 807,500 records, monthly updates (Information Access Company, Belmont, CA)

The NATIONAL NEWSPAPER INDEX provides front-to-back indexing of the Christian Science Monitor, the New York Times, and the Wall Street Journal. All articles, news reports, editorials, letters to the editor, obituaries, product evaluations, biographical pieces, poetry, recipes, columns, cartoons and illustrations, and reviews are included. The only items not included are weather charts, stock market tables, crossword puzzles, and horoscopes. In addition, the NATIONAL NEWSPAPER INDEX indexes national and international news stories written by the staff writers of the Washington Post and the Los Angeles Times. Other types of articles from these two papers are indexed selectively.

-5-

The NATIONAL NEWSPAPER INDEX, particularly useful for answering general news and business questions, provides a valuable adjunct in such areas as market research, public relations, government relations, journalism, food and nutrition, and the social sciences.

$84 per online connect hour, 20¢ per full record printed offline, 10¢ per full record typed or displayed online. (DIALOG File 111)

11/84
/caec

ERIC AVAILABLE ON PERSONAL COMPUTERS

Personal computer users may now access the entire ERIC database through
three "user friendly" database vendor services: Dialog's "Knowledge Index,"
BRS's "BRS/After Dark," and CompuServe. These services offer database access
through simplified search strategies: simplified combination and limiting
commands, and free text searching through a single key word or phrase rather
than ERIC descriptors. Generally, service is limited to evening and weekend
hours, is offered at relatively low cost, and is billed through major credit
cards. For information on how to program a personal computer to emulate
a computer terminal, see the ERIC Digest, "Accessing ERIC with Your Microcomputer."

•Dialog's Knowledge Index is designed to provide home
or personal computer users with a simplified version of
Dialog's search capabilities and low-cost access to a selected
group of files, including ERIC. In addition to a $35 initial
subscription fee, there is a $24/hour charge for all files.
There is no minimum monthly usage charge. Knowledge Index
is available between 6 p.m. and 5 a.m. Monday-Friday; 8 a.m.
until midnight on Saturday; and 3 p.m. Sunday until 5 a.m.
Monday. For more information, contact Dialog/Knowledge
Index at (800) 528-6050, ext. 415.

•BRS/After Dark is a user-friendly system developed
by Bibliographic Retrieval Services (BRS) to allow home
or personal computer users to access ERIC and other databases
between 6 p.m. and midnight. Rates include a one-time
subscription fee of $50 plus a $6/hour charge. There is
a $12 per month minimum usage fee. Individual database
royalties have been reduced and are not included in the
$6 per connect hour charge. Subscribers are billed through
their bank credit cards. Further information can be obtained
by calling BRS/After Dark at (800) 833-4707.

•To access ERIC on CompuServe, computer owners must
first purchase a "starter kit" (available at retail stores
for approximately $40). These kits include a temporary
user ID, temporary password, and a user's guide. Computer
users may log on using this starter kit and once connected,
enter name, and billing information to obtain a regular
CompuServe subscription. Once subscribed, the user may
access general information about the ERIC system as well
as the ERIC database itself. At present, users can access
only ERIC documents and journal titles and code numbers
(ED and EJ numbers) on Compuserve. They must then locate
and read the ERIC abstracts in Resources in Education and
Current Index to Journals in Education at a library with
an ERIC collection. In the future, ERIC abstracts and
ordering information should be available through CompuServe.
For further information, write CompuServe, 1200 Chambers
Road, Columbus, OH 43212.

-2-

In addition to the above services, selective collections of ERIC documents
are available to personal computer users in software packages. While these
do not provide access to the entire ERIC collection, they are useful in
school settings for teaching faculty and students about the ERIC system,
computerized databases, and computer search strategy. Each provides access
to ERIC citations through the use of simplified commands and free text searching using key words rather than ERIC descriptors.

    •On August 1, 1982, the ERIC Clearinghouse on Information
Resources began offering subscriptions to MICROsearch,
a computer program used to search specially prepared disketts
containing small related segments of the ERIC database.
Designed for use by those without training in online searching, MICROsearch requires an Apple II Plus microcomputer
with a minimum of 48K Ram, Apple DOS 3.3 operating system,
and at least one disc drive. Each database diskette contains
200 to 300 bibliographic records on a particular subject
area selected from Resources in Education (RIE) and Current
Index to Journals in Education (CIJE). Quarterly updates
will contain two to three diskettes at $6 per diskette.
The first two subjects available are Educational Technology
and Library and Information Science. A demonstration set
including one diskette of MICROsearch software, a sample
database diskette, and a manual is available for $10.
For information, contact the ERIC Clearinghouse on Information Resources, School of Education, Syracuse University,
Syracuse, NY 13210 (315) 423-3640.

    •EASYsearch Resources in a Nutshell. This microcomputer
based search program is designed for K-12 teachers with
no prior experience in database searching. It consists
of a reproducible program disk and seven separate database
diskettes. Each diskette focuses on a specific subject
area: social studies, reading/literature, language arts,
math, and science. It should be noted that this is a commercial
program and has not been developed by ERIC. For each diskette,
the publishers have selected journal and document citations
from the ERIC database which they consider to be of particular
use to the elementary or secondary practitioner. An update
service is also available to schools wishing to receive
new citations as they are entered into the ERIC system.
For more information, contact Renaissance Learning Systems,
Tecumseh Building, Jamesville, NY 13078.

-3-

Book Tells How to Search ERIC with Computers. One of the most popular ERIC publications, <u>How to Prepare for a Computer Search of ERIC: A Non-Technical Approach</u>, has been revised and updated. The 1983 edition, by Marilyn Laubacher, is a comprehensive revision of the original 1975 edition by Judith Yarborough.

The publication is designed for educators and other individuals who want to develop search strategies for using ERIC. Nontechnical language guides the user through the search process in a step-by-step fashion from initiation to implementation.

Appendices provide descriptions of other databases of interest to educators, publication types and codes, and a complete list of educational level descriptors. A glossary is included.

The publication is available from Information Resources Publications, Syracuse University, School of Education, 030 Huntington Hall, Syracuse, NY 13210 for $3.75 plus $1.50 for postage and handling.

11/84
/caec

INDEX